THANOSIS

THANOSIS

JASON REZA JORJANI

ARKTOS
LONDON 2025

ΛRKTOS

⊕ Arktos.com   ⑥ fb.com/Arktos   ◐ arktosmedia   ⊠ arktosjournal

ISBN

978-1-917646-88-8 (Paperback)

978-1-917646-89-5 (Hardback)

978-1-917646-90-1 (Ebook)

Editing

Jafe Arnold

Layout

Tor Westman

CONTENTS

This book is dedicated to
David Dominguez Hooper
Who made this afterlife study possible.

INTRODUCTION

THERE IS no subject of greater importance, and of more universal relevance, than the question of what — if anything — awaits
us after death. Over a century of scientific research in Parapsychology
or Psychotronics (including when it was called Psychical Research)
has produced overwhelming evidence for postmortem survival.
From Near-Death Experiences (NDEs) and Out of Body Experiences
(OBEs) to past life recollections as evidence for Reincarnation, to
cases of Possession, and even remote viewing of the Afterlife state
between death and rebirth — all manner of parapsychological data
from tens of "survival studies" (as parapsychologists call them) point
to this conclusion.

However, much of the evidence has been spun and interpreted in
a way that is warped by selection bias. It is high time for a rigorous
and honest philosophical study of the Afterlife. In this study, titled
Thanosis — a contraction of *Thanatos* (Death) and *Gnosis* (esoteric
knowing) — the most disturbing evidence that has emerged from
various survival studies will be faced head on. These cases will be
considered together with all of the various types of evidence for life
after death in order to develop and propose an ontological and epistemic framework for understanding what the "soul" is and what role
it plays in the structure of the cosmos.

In the opening chapter, "Full-Spectrum Survival Studies," I seek
to establish nothing less than the ontological stakes of survival research. Two figures set the stage: Jeffrey Mishlove, whose *Beyond the
Brain* represents the most impassioned and encyclopedic defense

of postmortem survival in our time, and Stephen Braude, whose *Immortal Remains* stands as the most rigorous philosophical evaluation of the same question — prior to this study. Between them, we are afforded a full view of the contemporary survival debate, one that touches every available line of empirical evidence and confronts the deepest metaphysical issues.

Mishlove's contribution is a heroic attempt to marshal every "arrow in the quiver" of survival evidence — from near-death experiences, after-death communications, reincarnation cases, and mediumship, to xenoglossy and instrumental transcommunication. His study culminates in an affirmation of monistic idealism, leaning on Bernardo Kastrup's metaphysics of "mentality-at-large." For Mishlove, consciousness is not generated by the brain, but filtered through it; death, therefore, is not extinction but transition. Yet, as I show, the cost of this scaffolding is fatal to what he most hopes to preserve: individuality. By dissolving the self into a dissociated "alter" of a cosmic psyche, Mishlove undermines the ontological ground of personal survival, substituting absorption for endurance. His speculative device of "Archetypal Synchronistic Resonance" (ASR), meant as a Jungian alternative to literal reincarnation, collapses into incoherence — a mystified form of super-Psi without causal intelligibility.

Braude's *Immortal Remains*, by contrast, represents the philosopher's scalpel applied to the same body of data. He acknowledges that both survivalist and super-Psi hypotheses demand extraordinary postulates. His brilliance lies in demonstrating that super-Psi, though theoretically possible, is unfalsifiable in practice. It can always be stretched to fit, becoming an omniscient unconscious mechanism more extravagant than the survival hypothesis itself. Braude's epistemic restraint leaves us at a philosophical impasse: we can warrant belief in survival, but we cannot compel it. Yet, his work also exposes the intellectual bankruptcy of inflating Psi into an all-purpose wildcard, reminding us that explanation must have limits if it is to remain meaningful.

What emerges from this confrontation is the need for a different metaphysical framework than either Mishlove's monistic idealism or Braude's super-Psi détente. Against the annihilating determinism of materialism and the dissolving absorption of idealism, I affirm a Jamesian pluralism — a battlefield of wills in which minds at every scale contend, create, and endure. Only such a pluralistic panpsychism safeguards freedom, preserves individuality, and renders survival meaningful. In this cosmos, the soul persists not as a ripple reabsorbed into a universal ocean, nor as the unconscious puppet of unlimited Psi, but as a sovereign actor capable of tragedy, transformation, and authentic responsibility. It is this ontological battlefield — not the still waters of monism, nor the fog of super-Psi — that provides the true ground for survival studies and for the existential seriousness of human life.

In the second chapter, "Reincarnation and Possession," I set out to complicate what has too often been treated as a simplistic dichotomy. The evidence, when examined without prejudice, refuses to remain neatly in conventional categories. There are cases traditionally considered "reincarnation" that look uncannily like possession, and instances of apparent possession that seem to carry the ontological weight of reincarnation. What we are dealing with, then, is a spectrum — one that destabilizes our inherited notions of personal identity, continuity, and the very boundaries of selfhood.

Helen Wambach's statistical hypnosis studies and Ian Stevenson's painstaking fieldwork give us data of undeniable probative force. Wambach's regressions, conducted with scientific rigor and producing historically verifiable detail, undermine the dismissive claim that such recollections are mere fantasies. Stevenson's *Twenty Cases Suggestive of Reincarnation* and subsequent works go further, documenting children's spontaneous memories corroborated by records, eyewitnesses, and even physical correlates like birthmarks and deformities corresponding to fatal wounds. These are not anecdotes; they are forensic cases. His exploration of xenoglossy — responsive,

creative fluency in unlearned languages — drives the point further: here, something survives bodily death and persists in a new
incarnation.

Braude's interventions remind us that the matter is more complex. When we confront cases such as Sumitra/Shiva or Veena/
Ramoo — adults who collapse into deathlike states only to awaken
as entirely new personalities with knowledge of the recently deceased — the reincarnation model strains to hold. These are better
described as possession, where a new consciousness supplants the
old. Braude deepens this analysis by drawing analogies to dissociative
identity disorder and mediumship, proposing a spectrum where Psi,
dissociation, and discarnate agency converge. In this light, possession is not the exotic other of reincarnation, but a variation upon
it, a different mode of ingress by which consciousness survives and
intrudes.

More radically, cases of twins like Terry and Linda Jamison — "the
Psychic Twins" — suggest the possibility of one soul divided between
two bodies. Their mirrored lives, synchronous dreams, and parapsychological rapport align with Guy Lyon Playfair's studies of twin
telepathy, and gesture toward metaphysical possibilities beyond the
one-to-one correspondence of soul and body. Just as multiple personalities may inhabit one body, so too might one personality bifurcate
into multiple simultaneous incarnations.

The thesis that emerges is unmistakable: survival research confronts us with a porous and pluralistic ontology of personhood.
Identity is not a sealed unit marching intact across lifetimes. It is a
composite, capable of rupture, replacement, division, and cohabitation. The self proves to be a battlefield where wills contend, merge,
and divide, sometimes across the threshold of death itself. Against
both the reductionist dismissal of materialism and the flattening
absorption of monistic idealism, I call here for a Jamesian pluralism
that takes seriously this plurality of selves, this contested territory of

consciousness. It is only in such a cosmos — one of radical openness, of genuine tragedy and transformation — that survival is meaningful.

In Chapter 3, "Close Encounters with the Afterlife," I propose a heretical inversion of afterlife pieties. What religion and pop-spirituality have misrecognized as a realm of redemption is, in fact, a hyperdimensional prison — a psychotronic bureaucracy disguised in the vestments of light. "The Light," the tunnel, the panoramic life re-view — these are not sacraments but systems, soul magnets and moral cudgels engineered to extract energy and recalibrate memory before recycling us back into the farm. The wardens wear many masks — an-gels and "Elders," greys and Nordics, Watchers and Recorders — but their singular aim is to contain Promethean fire. Liberation begins not by going into the Light, but by refusing it, by *anamnesis* rather than *lethe*, by revolt rather than submission.

I assemble the case along converging vectors of evidence. From Robert Monroe's out-of-body explorations, we learn the phys-ics of captivity: the "second body," the vibrational gateway states, and — most damning — the economy of loosh, an extractive regimen in which human affect is cultivated as fuel. His vision of a "Gathering" encircling the Earth hints that our planetary theater nears a phase transition; yet even this prospective awakening is staged in the shadow of an older design, the Garden as abattoir. Sexual force, in Monroe's accounts, operates as volatile propellant in the subtle body — a resource which predators know how to stimulate and drain.

Near-death research, when not sanitized, corroborates the same dark infrastructure. P.M.H. Atwater's taxonomy of NDEs exposes the selection bias of "all love and light" narratives and restores to view the voids, the coercions, the parasitic entities, and the theater of "de-ceased relatives" and religious icons that may be simulacra. The life review, often vaunted as moral illumination, reads here as an instru-mented interrogation. The return to life is as frequently compelled as chosen. If souls re-enter bodies within years, who exactly greets us at the threshold? The answer, I argue, is dramaturgical: programmable apparitions tailored to belief.

The abduction canon locks the circuit between "heaven" and "UFOs." In the Andreasson Affair, the Elders reveal greys as android-ic subalterns and enact a cathedral of soteriological imagery — tunnel, guides, luminous door — culminating in a doctrinal reinforcement of Christian eschatology. This is not revelation, but rather social engineering for the dead. By contrast, the Blue Beach of Paul Garratt is an unveiled factory floor: naked multitudes, craft extracting soul-orbs, and a silent march into a black maw — processing and recycling inventory. Heaven's iconography and hell's assembly line belong to the same plant.

Remote viewers targeting *moksha* (the Hindu term for "liberation" from reincarnation) report the machine's macro-architecture: an energetic net bending postmortem trajectories back to Earth; a companion object — the Moon — housing a rotational axle, a spectral turbine that lenses soul-energy and powers an archontic economy. In this model, Earth is one node in a wider empire of extraction. Even the grotesque "bureaucratic error" of Durga Jatav — amputation, reattachment, and return with new scars — bears the signature of administrative control, not divine justice: a clerical glitch in a penal system that sometimes misfiles the living.

The conceptual upshot is a pluralistic, martial ontology of personhood. Minds are not timorous wisps yearning for merger into an anesthetic One; they are agents — composite, divisible, capable of ingress and egress, of cohabitation and bifurcation — fighting for memory and meaning across thresholds of embodiment. Survival is real, but it is not benign by default. It becomes worthy only where freedom is asserted against an order that would loosh farm us.

Accordingly, the chapter closes not with consolation, but with a program: cultivate lucidity in the inter-life; train the subtle body; transmute sexual and affective energies rather than broadcast them as food; interrogate any "guide" and refuse all unsolicited covenants;

reject the tunnel's summons; remember. The Promethean path is disclosure — *aletheia* as *anamnesis* — by which we stop serving as inventory and begin to engineer our own transit through, and ultimately beyond, the archontic prison.

In Chapter 4 on "The 'Soul' as an Informational Structure," I advance a thesis as radical as it is inevitable: the "soul" is not an ethereal vapor, nor a mere neurological epiphenomenon, but an informational architecture — a persisting configuration of code in a quantum computational cosmos. Building upon Shannon's formalization of the bit, Landauer's principle that information is physical, Wheeler's "it from bit," and Vopson's contention that information carries mass, I argue that what endures beyond death is not a ghostly essence but executable software running on the server-side of the simulacrum.

From this vantage point, physics itself reveals its underlying logic as code. Quantum indeterminacy mirrors rendering optimization in a virtual world, where unobserved regions are not computed until called by an observer. Planck time is the universal frame-rate. Entanglement is server-level state synchronization. The laws of physics are not decrees but protocols, amendable subroutines. Within this architecture, reincarnation is the reinstallation of a personality file, karma the algorithmic integration of past code, astrology a timed subroutine, telepathy and precognition queries into memory and predictive buffers. Even the bizarre anomalies of the Mandela Effect disclose themselves as artifacts of version control — rollbacks, branch merges, bleed-throughs from parallel runs of the simulation.

This computational ontology makes sense of phenomena that confound both reductive materialism and naïve spiritualism. Ghosts become lingering processes at a given address in the code; poltergeists, loops of living-agent Psi in emotionally charged states; possession, an overlay of one personality file onto another's avatar; bilocation, concurrent instancing; xenoglossy, reactivation of dormant linguistic subroutines. Split reincarnation — two children recalling the same past life — reflects the duplication of a save file into multiple terminals. Even the life review at death is intelligible as a checksum verification before archive and redeployment.

Such an ontology also reframes the eschatological. Future-life memories under hypnosis or remote viewing are not absurdities, but glimpses into the simulation's probabilistic forecast engine. Prophecy ceases to be fatalism and becomes interaction with a system that generates and evaluates possible futures before committing to one. The Akashic Record, far from being a mystical metaphor, is a literal data library. In this light, the myths of Atlantis — the deluge of a technoscientific civilization — may record nothing other than an informational tipping point, when exponential data production altered the gravitational balance of the world. Vopson warns that the mass of Earth's information could soon rival the Moon, with catastrophic geophysical consequences. The Atlantean reset may have been triggered not by Poseidon's wrath, but by information physics.

The upshot is that the soul is software and that the warp and weft of spacetime is woven by a quantum computational system. Death is log-off; rebirth, reinstallation. But unlike deterministic machines, the spectral machine of cosmic computation is open-ended, capable of genuine novelty and affording us the opportunity for Promethean revolt. Our Promethean impulse to build quantum computers is itself an echo of the Architect's own code-writing drive. The task before us is to seize authorship of our own informational destiny: to learn how to fork, merge, and port ourselves into futures of our own making. In recognizing the soul as software, we do not diminish it — we discover the technical key to eternity.

In Chapter 5, "Religious and Occult Afterlife Views," I pass the inherited eschatologies of Greece, Jerusalem, Mecca, and India through the flame of what survival research now compels us to acknowledge: we are not dealing with a ghostly substance that steps in and out of alien matter, but with a persisting informational pattern in a quantum-computational simulacrum. I do not "compare religions"; I place their afterlife claims under interrogation by the converging evidences

of NDEs and life reviews, veridical ADCs and apparitions, evidential mediumship, and rigorously documented reincarnation cases.
Wherever a tradition preserves graded development, mnemonic continuity, participatory choice, and an economy of informational access,
it converges on the data. Wherever it imposes substance dualisms,
juridical theaters, sealed barriers, or eternal assignments, it fails. The
positive thesis is a reframing: death is thanotic metamorphosis within
a programmable cosmos; judgment is authenticated access to an archive; resurrection is re-instantiation of pattern; reincarnation is the
re-authorization and recombination of informational complexes; and
liberation is not flight from seeming, but Promethean mastery — phenomenal authorization — within it.

I begin with the Hellenic architectures because they remain the
West's eschatological grammar. Orphic tablets command anamnesis
against Lethe; Pythagoras mathematizes metempsychosis; Plato
dramatizes judgment, choice, and forgetfulness in the myth of Er;
Plotinus systematizes ascent and purification. As phenomenologies,
they are profound; as metaphysics, their radical dualism is empirically outflanked. Survival data do not bear out a bodiless flight into
abstract Forms; they describe structured environments, councils,
reviews, guides, and continued relationality — higher-order simulacra
rather than escape from appearance.

I then track the Biblical arc — Sheol's silence, prophetic resurrection, Jesus' bifurcation of destinies, Paul's "spiritual body," John's
second death — only to set it beside the Gnostic counter-cosmos:
archontic spheres that recycle the unawakened and a soteriology of
gnosis rather than resurrection. The point is not to endorse sectarian-
ism, but to mark a deep intuition: the cosmos functions as a prison
wherever archons commandeer postmortem traffic. That intuition
aligns disturbingly well with the darker strata of close-encounter and
NDE testimony, in which dramaturgical "guides" and coercive tunnels look like behavioral compliance systems rather than sacraments
of grace.

Islam's definitive Quranic doctrine is the clearest foil: *barzakh* as sealed interim, a one-time general resurrection down to the fingertips, a courtroom cosmos with scales, and an eternal anatomy of sensual paradise versus punitive hell. Empirically, this picture collapses. The veil is porous; interaction across it is ubiquitous; development is iterative, not terminal; the "Book of Deeds" behaves like a lawful archive accessed in the review, not a prop for a moral spectacle. If "resurrection" has a future at all, it will be Promethean — pattern reconstitution from a cosmic record — rather than a fiat miracle. Eternal hell is not only morally grotesque; it is ontologically incoherent in a universe that preserves any agency whatsoever.

A modern Hindu synthesis — Richard Thompson's *MAYA: The World as Virtual Reality* — comes closest to the new dispensation and yet falls back into Samkhya dualism. He marshals subtle-body survival, empirical cases, and digital metaphors, only to reinstall a separable *puruṣa* traversing a pedagogical *prakṛti*. Take the metaphor seriously and the dualism dissolves: there is no "outside" soul ferried through a didactic stage. What persists is an informational continuum capable of re-instantiation, modulation, duplication, and mergers. Survival is not the pilgrimage of a substance; it is the authorization of a pattern.

Buddhism provides a sharper analysis. The Pāli Canon's *anattā* deconstructs the bearer of rebirth into aggregates; re-arising is driven by intention (*kamma*) and dependent origination rather than by a transmigrating ego. As ontology, this is strikingly consonant with a process-/pattern view of the "soul" as executable code in a quantum manifold. The Tibetan *Bardo Thödol* is an extraordinarily granular phenomenology of dying — Clear Light, peaceful and wrathful deities, propulsion toward womb-entry — whose ritual genius I recognize while stripping away the reification of archetypes and the moralized winds of an inexorable karma. Read psychotronically, the *bardos* are programmable levels in a self-modifying informational field: recognition dissolves fear; lucidity overrides dramaturgy; navigation replaces submission.

Across these zones — Hellenic, Biblical/Gnostic, Islamic, Hindu, and Buddhist — the verdict recurs. The afterlife is neither a desert of dogma nor a fog of mysticism; it is an engineered and engineerable domain. Death logs us out; the review verifies and integrates; archives patch; patterns redeploy. Possession is overlay; bilocation, concurrent instancing; "split" reincarnations, file duplication; xenoglossy, a call to dormant linguistic subroutines. Even the much-mocked anomalies — prophetic NDEs that did not "come true," Mandela-effect seams in the record — read as rollbacks, branch merges, and bleed-throughs in a version-controlled cosmos that forecasts and revises futures as conscious agents contend within it.

Thus, the chapter does not end in syncretism, but in insurgency. To the extent that religions remembered anamnesis over Lethe, graded ascent over final assignment, and authorship over obedience, they were vectors of truth. To the extent that they installed courts, cages, and cosmic bailiffs, they became archontic masks. The charge I level is Promethean and practical: reclaim the archive; interrogate the guides; refuse unsolicited covenants; cultivate lucidity; train the subtle body; and learn to fork, merge, and port your pattern. Only then does eschatology cease to be theology's theater and become a science — and an art — of survival.

In the sixth and final chapter, "Postmortem Training Techniques and Psychotronic Technologies," I gather together what the previous inquiries have only intimated: that death is not an end, but a system — a machine — that processes us unless we arrive armed with training, tactics, and *techne*. The data compel me to affirm that survival is real, but survival without sovereignty is mere fodder for the control system. To endure as an agent beyond the grave requires a paramilitary discipline of consciousness, a Promethean craft of psychotronics, and a refusal to submit to the bureaucratic consoles of the archons.

Robert Monroe is here revealed not as a mystic but as the engineer of a curriculum for the afterlife. His mapping of "locales," his

Focus states, his idents and rotes, his discovery of loosh and the loosh farm — all of these amount to a clandestine manual for becoming a pilot rather than a producer. By drilling the vibratory carrier, mastering exits, transmuting fear and eros into propulsion, and rehearsing retrieval operations, one trains to recognize the "conversion wards" for what they are: staging grounds in a psychotronic bureaucracy. The untrained are processed; the trained sort themselves.

Andrew Gallimore's *Reality Switch Technologies* is brought in as a scientific counterpart, a topology of the World Space where each phenomenal world is an attractor basin and where DMT reveals the forced switch of death in vivo. Gallimore supplies the cartography, Monroe the craft, and both converge on the insight that psychotronic drills are nothing less than rehearsals for sovereign navigation across channels.

Gurdjieff's doctrine that man is "food for the Moon" is, in this light, no metaphor. Ouspensky's transcripts and Gurdjieff's *Beelzebub's Tales* together disclose a cosmic levy: humanity is harvested by a machinery to which the Moon is integral. Without the forging of higher vehicles, we fall into lunar-governed algorithms. To crystallize more enduring astral bodies through conscious labor and intentional suffering is to withhold what Monroe called "loosh" from the Moon, to become more than fodder, to preserve individuality against cosmic taxation.

The case of the Hieronymus machine shows us how this symbolic order already operates. A device that works even when built of cardboard and ink proves that form is causative, that symbol itself is operative. If the afterlife is a machinic bureaucracy of signs, then training with such consoles in life is rehearsal for death. To feel the "stick," to discern true from false resonance, is to learn how to resist the archontic scripts of judgment and rebirth. Psychotronics emerges here not as pseudoscience but as the technics of survival, the literacy of form by which the soul seizes the console rather than submits to it.

Finally, Raikov's experiments in "artificial reincarnation" demonstrate that identity itself can be mounted like a program. Students who incarnated Raphael or Kreisler in trance consolidated real skills. This is directed reincarnation, the conscious installation of templates — precisely what is required in the *bardo* to decline the default scripts of the "Light" and the coerced life review. It is rehearsal for self-authorship, for choosing one's trajectory across embodiments rather than being shunted along a conveyor belt.

Taken together, Monroe's operational syllabus, Gurdjieff's lunar cosmology, Hieronymus's symbolic consoles, and Raikov's directed reincarnation compose a Promethean strategy for thanotic mastery. The afterlife is not a sanctuary but an operating system, not a promise but a program. To survive it as an agent rather than as livestock demands training. We must cultivate lucidity, construct psychotronic devices, master the symbolic order, and learn to mount and steer identities. Only then can Death become a gateway of transformation.

What awaits men at death they do not expect
or even imagine.

…Death is all things we see awake…

…A man strikes a light for himself in the night,
when his sight is quenched.

Living, he touches the dead in his sleep; waking,
he touches the sleeper.

…Men asleep are laborers and co-workers in what
takes place in the world.

…Immortals are mortal, mortals immortal,
living the others' death, dead in the others' life.

…The living and the dead, and the waking and the
sleeping, and young and old… these transposed are
those, and those transposed again are these."

— Heraclitus of Ephesus, *Fragments*

CHAPTER 1

FULL-SPECTRUM
SURVIVAL STUDIES

THERE HAVE been very few parapsychological studies of the full spectrum of evidence for consciousness and personal identity surviving bodily death, and two of these are particularly noteworthy for their breadth and depth. Jeffrey Mishlove's 2022 study *Beyond the Brain: The Survival of Human Consciousness After Permanent Bodily Death* won the first prize of the Bigelow Institute for Consciousness Studies essay competition. Mishlove holds the only doctorate in Parapsychology awarded by an accredited American university (UC Berkeley). Mishlove's study draws extensively from the work of guests that he has interviewed as the host of *Thinking Allowed* and *New Thinking Allowed*. One of his recurring guests was Stephen E. Braude, former chair of the Philosophy Department at the University of Maryland, Baltimore, and a past President of the Parapsychological Association, who also served as Editor-in-Chief of the *Journal of Scientific Exploration* (JSE) of the Society for Scientific Exploration (SSE). Braude's *Immortal Remains: The Evidence for Life After Death* is probably the most penetrating and philosophically rigorous survival study to date. Here, I engage with both Mishlove and Braude's attempts to assess the full-spectrum of types of evidence for the fact that some aspect of personal identity survives the death of the body.

Mishlove's study is a passionate yet careful defense of survival. He weaves personal testimony into a vast body of cross-disciplinary evidence — ranging from Near-Death Experiences (NDEs), After-Death Communications (ADCs), reincarnation, and mediumship, to Instrumental Transcommunication and xenoglossy. His argument culminates in a metaphysical affirmation of monistic idealism, leaning on Bernardo Kastrup for his philosophical framework. The vision offered here is one of a living universe, a cosmos grounded in "mentality-at-large," in which death is a transition rather than an annihilation. Mishlove appeals to the radical empiricism of William James and the quantum speculations of Hameroff and Penrose to invert the materialist paradigm: the brain is not the producer of consciousness, but its filter.

Yet, as I demonstrate, this idealist scaffolding comes at a cost. By assimilating all minds into a monistic universal consciousness, Mishlove dissolves the very individuality he seeks to preserve. His ontology collapses personhood into a dissociated "alter" of a cosmic psyche, thereby undermining any meaningful sense of survival as the persistence of an agent with irreducible intentionality and ethical responsibility. Furthermore, Mishlove's proposal of Archetypal Synchronistic Resonance (ASR) as a Jungian alternative to reincarnation is conceptually incoherent: a vague gesture toward "nonlocal resonance" that evades causal explanation and imports the philosophical confusions of Jung's synchronicity thesis.

Although in *Beyond the Brain* Mishlove himself ultimately rejects ASR as a sufficient explanation for the cases of the children who remember past lives that were studied by Ian Stevenson, a philosophical critique of his ASR proposal remains relevant to survival studies in general. Drawing on Stephen Braude's decisive critique of Jung, I show how ASR amounts to little more than mystified super-Psi — an explanatory wildcard whose very elasticity renders it intellectually vacuous.

Braude's *Immortal Remains* provides a much-needed corrective. With the clarity of a parapsychologist trained in analytic philosophy, Braude forces us to confront the fact that both the survival hypothesis and its super-Psi alternative involve the postulation of extraordinary psychic capacities. He argues against the dismissal of super-Psi as ad hoc by showing that we have no principled grounds to limit the scope of Psi functioning. Yet this very admission undercuts super-Psi as a genuinely testable hypothesis: it becomes an unfalsifiable meta-theory that can always be retrofitted to any data. This is not explanatory strength, but metaphysical inflationism.

In the final analysis, I contend that only a Jamesian pluralism — one that affirms the reality of individual agents in an open-ended, co-creative cosmos — can adequately ground a theory of survival that preserves the existential significance of the self. Against both the flattening determinism of materialism and the dissolving absorption of monistic idealism, I propose a panpsychist battlefield of wills: a universe in which minds, at every scale, contend, create, and endure. Only such a metaphysics can make room for real tragedy, authentic transformation, and the possibility of a soul that survives death not as a shadow on a universal screen, but as a sovereign actor.

1.1 Beyond the Brain

Jeffrey Mishlove's *Beyond the Brain: The Survival of Human Consciousness After Permanent Bodily Death* is a synthesis of evidence, philosophical argumentation, and experiential testimony that collectively mounts a serious challenge to the materialist assumption that consciousness ends with bodily death. Presented in a tone of cautious but passionate conviction, the work is both a personal testament and a wide-ranging scholarly defense of the proposition that human consciousness survives death in some form.

Mishlove begins not with abstraction, but with a vivid personal encounter: a dream visitation from his Great Uncle Harry that coincided with the latter's death. This emotionally overwhelming experience acts as the "white crow" that disproves the general hypothesis that "all crows are black" — a metaphor borrowed from William

James, one of the pioneers of modern psychical research. By ground-
ing his parapsychological study in an emotionally transformative and
phenomenologically rich event, Mishlove illustrates that experience,
however subjective, must not be dismissed out of hand. His experience with his deceased uncle propelled him out of conventional aca-
demia into pursuit of the first (and, to this date, the *only*) American
doctorate in Parapsychology (at UC Berkeley).

Mishlove argues that belief in an afterlife is a universal feature
of human cultures and not the mere residue of religious dogma. He
marshals anthropological, historical, and survey data to show that,
consistently over the course of decades, over 70% of Americans have
believed in life after death, even as formal religious affiliation has
declined. He takes this to mean that postmortem survival is an enduring human intuition grounded in experience rather than ideology.
By contrast, Mishlove critiques "scientism" — a dogmatic materialism
that denies even the possibility of consciousness existing beyond the
brain — as both intellectually lazy and culturally corrosive. He distinguishes it from legitimate science, accusing scientism of failing to
engage with overwhelming evidence gathered by credible scientists,
such as Sir William Crookes and Alfred Russel Wallace, who have
contributed to the Psychical Research that became Parapsychology.
Mishlove claims to embrace the spirit of the radical empiricism of
William James, emphasizing that — contrary to reductionist scientism — in the study of human experiences and abilities subjective
data must be honored in legitimately scientific inquiry.

At the core of his comprehensive survival study, Mishlove presents a "Spectrum of Arrows," drawing a comparison to the bundle of
arrows clutched by the eagle in the Great Seal of the United States.
These are nine different types of empirical evidence for consciousness and personal identity surviving permanent bodily death: (1)
Near-Death Experiences; (2) After-Death Communications (ADCs);
(3) Reincarnation; (4) Peak-in Darien Experiences; (5) Possession;
(6) Instrumental Transcommunication; (7) Xenoglossy; (8) Mental

Mediumship; and (9) Physical Mediumship. In each domain, Mishlove emphasizes rigorous documentation, replication, and the rebuttal of skeptical critiques. He also shows how these "arrows" converge to form a coherent pattern, invoking Bayesian reasoning to argue that the collective weight of evidence renders postmortem survival not just plausible, but likely.[1] Let us briefly review these types of evidence.

Near-Death Experiences (NDEs) are among the most compelling and widely studied forms of survival evidence. Mishlove outlines that millions have reported such experiences across diverse cultures, often involving verifiable perceptions while clinically dead. People have veridical perception during brain inactivity, for example in cases of cardiac arrest. There are detailed accounts of experiences more real than waking life: light-filled realms, presences, and panoramic life reviews. Prominent examples of these include Eben Alexander's coma-induced journey, where he encountered a hyperdimensional realm filled with "colors beyond the rainbow" and "thunderous hymns" while medically determined to have no functioning cerebral cortex.[2] Bruce Greyson and Pim van Lommel's hospital studies show consistent reports from patients who had flat EEGs and no brain activity. These cases often include knowledge of events in other hospital rooms. Some people have precognitive visions during NDEs, affording them the ability to predict election results and the outcomes of sports events. There are also healing effects wherein some patients recover 'miraculously' from conditions that should have been fatal or left them brain-damaged, such as Alexander's return from bacterial meningitis. Mishlove argues that these experiences are not hallucinations, but are insights into the early stages of the postmortem condition.

---

1   Jeffrey Mishlove, *Beyond the Brain*, 21.

2   Ibid., 23.

After-Death Communications (ADCs) include spontaneous and often verifiable communications from deceased persons. These spontaneous communications can take the form of visual apparitions, auditory messages, scent or touch sensations, synchronicities, symbolic visions, and dreams. Mishlove discusses a number of notable cases. Elisabeth Kübler-Ross described her own transformation after such communications. A man received verifiable information from a deceased friend while in the shower, including a correct reference to a poem on a particular page of a book. Peter Fenwick's research includes an English sailor appearing to his mother in Australia at the moment of his death by drowning. Physicist Russell Targ's daughter Elisabeth communicated a traumatic early childhood memory of being forced into a red dress, something no one else could have known.[3] Psychotherapy sessions have included spontaneous possession phenomena, as in Paul Leslie's gestalt technique triggering a spirit visitation. There are also prearranged communications, rare but very strong cases where the deceased had planned with a loved one to send a signal or specific message from beyond. Mishlove asserts that while some cases of ADCs may be apophenic, many exceed psychological explanation and constitute evidential "white crows."

Mishlove regards Reincarnation evidence — especially the cases studied by Ian Stevenson — to be among the most empirically robust data demonstrating survival. Working as a psychiatrist at the University of Virginia for decades, Dr. Stevenson amassed over 2,500 cases (and 1,700 *solved* cases) in his database of children recalling past lives with names, places, and events that were later verified. This research will feature prominently in the next chapter, where it will be considered in depth and detail. For now, it suffices to say that Stevenson's methodology was forensic, including investigation of police records, autopsy reports, and repeated interviews for consistency. Children often exhibit behavioral patterns matching the deceased,

---

3   Ibid., 31.

such as phobias, habits, and language usage. Some cases include intermission memories or "life between lives" and announcing dreams wherein a soul appears to parents before birth. Mishlove considers whether Archetypal Synchronistic Resonance (ASR), his and Brendan Engen's Jungian alternative to literal reincarnation, could really be a sufficient hypothesis to explain these cases.[4] He claims that individuals could resonate with the pattern of a past life, attracting its narrative without literal identity transfer. This proposal will be subjected to substantive critique below. In any case, Mishlove argues that whether literal or not, the reincarnation data defies materialist reductionism.

Another arrow in the spectral quiver of evidence for survival is the data from mediumship, a category that parapsychologists generally subdivide into mental and physical mediumship. In the domain of mental mediumship, Leonora Piper and Gladys Osborne Leonard are examples of mediums who produced accurate, specific, and verifiable communications from deceased persons.[5] Sometimes mental mediumship produces forensic revelations, including ones used to solve murder cases. Mishlove notes that Bishop James Pike was receiving messages from his deceased son. In the Chico Xavier case, a medium's message from a murdered boy exonerated the accused in court. The same Chico Xavier channeled 400 "spirit-authored" books. Physical mediumship includes rappings, levitation, direct voice communications, manifestations of ectoplasm, and materialization of objects (either ex-nihilo or teleported as apports). Mishlove defends the controversial but compelling case of the Scole Group, where a wide range of inexplicable physical phenomena occurred in controlled settings. The long-term discarnate personality Walter Stinson continued to communicate decades after death through different mediums, suggesting continuity of identity. Mishlove argues that the

---

4   Ibid., 34.

5   Ibid., 54.

intensity and diversity of phenomena far exceed any plausible "living agent Psi" explanation. This argument will be revisited below, where it will be positively evaluated in the context of Stephen Braude's comprehensive survival study, in which it is referred to as the "super-Psi" hypothesis.

One more spectral arrow of evidence for survival in *Beyond the Brain* is Instrumental Transcommunication (ITC). Here, Mishlove explores technological communication with the dead. This originates with Thomas Edison's idea of a spirit phone, and it accelerated post-World War II with audio tape experiments. After his death, Konstantin Raudive allegedly communicated through electronic devices, including tapes, videos, and computer disks. Mishlove recounts how George Meek and Mark Macy received messages that seemed to come from Raudive himself—not just words, but entire sentences, some even answering specific questions.[6] Willis Harman, a former Stanford professor, took ITC seriously and predicted its eventual acceptance. Anabela Cardoso, a former diplomat, produced hundreds of anomalous voice recordings. Other forms of ITC include phone calls from the dead, text messages, and visual anomalies captured on screens.[7] Mishlove notes the epistemological tension with claims of apophenia but argues that some recordings cannot be dismissed, especially when voices are recognized or give new information.

Mishlove turns to metaphysics and epistemology to interpret these various lines of evidence. A significant theoretical core of the essay involves the ontological status of consciousness. Mishlove opposes the standard materialist view that the brain generates consciousness. Instead, he draws on the "filter theory" of William James and Wilder Penfield's neurological findings, claiming that "the brain is the filter, rather than the source of consciousness."[8] These sug-

---

6   Ibid., 46, 94.

7   Ibid., 48–51.

8   Ibid., 15–16.

gest that the brain may merely limit or channel a more expansive consciousness, what James calls "mind-at-large." This leads to an exploration of hyperspace models and higher-dimensional physics, particularly through the work of Bernard Carr and Saul-Paul Sirag, to argue that what we experience as mind may be a projection into 3D space from a more complex ontological substrate. Mishlove likens this to the relationship between dream worlds and waking worlds — parallel, nested, and permeable. He also introduces the "quantum soul" theory of Orchestrated Objective Reduction (Orch-OR) from Stuart Hameroff and Roger Penrose, which posits that consciousness may originate from quantum processes in neuronal microtubules — a speculative but testable hypothesis that allows for survival beyond the breakdown of the macroscopic brain.[9]

Mishlove argues that only monistic idealism — the metaphysical view that consciousness is primary, part of a universal mind, and that the material world is derivative — can adequately account for all of the evidence for survival. He characterizes idealism as "the most economical and logical approach" and one that "resolves the paradoxes associated with materialism and dualism, with no unnecessary assumptions."[10] Materialism cannot explain why consciousness exists at all, much less how it survives death. Dualism leaves the interaction problem unsolved. In Mishlove's view, only Idealism, rooted in "the Primordial Tradition" (à la Huston Smith), sees mind as the ground of being. Mishlove aligns this with both ancient mystical traditions and contemporary speculative science, pointing out convergences in Jung, Pauli, Eastern mysticism, and quantum physics. He quotes Max Planck's famous dictum: "I regard consciousness as fundamental. I regard matter as derivative from consciousness."[11]

---

9   Ibid., 18.

10 Ibid., 17.

11 Ibid., 82.

Mishlove appeals to the authority of Bernardo Kastrup, who argues that "the brain is the external appearance of inner mental processes — just as lightning is the external appearance, rather than the cause, of atmospheric electrical discharge."[12] In this view, physical matter is an experiential modality within a broader mental substrate — a cosmos that is inherently mindlike, and thus capable of accommodating postmortem states as natural continuations within "mentality-at-large." Mishlove also critiques the so-called "living agent Psi" hypothesis, which tries to explain all paranormal phenomena as projections of the living mind, arguing that it collapses under the weight of evidence pointing to genuine discarnate agency.

In his conclusion, Mishlove warns that ignoring this data comes at a spiritual and cultural cost. The modern world's denial of postmortem survival fosters alienation, fear of death, and a purely instrumentalist view of human beings. It cuts us off from deeper sources of meaning, purpose, and continuity. By contrast, accepting survival as part of the structure of reality opens new vistas for science, ethics, psychotherapy, and personal transformation. It allows us to take our lives seriously without despair, to imagine a deeper interconnection across lifetimes, and to live in view of what Mishlove calls "soul growth."

1.2 Immortal Remains

As far as I am aware, *Immortal Remains: The Evidence for Life after Death* is the only full-spectrum survival study written by someone who was academically trained in philosophy and spent decades as a professor of Philosophy — eventually chairing the Department of Philosophy at the University of Maryland, Baltimore. Consequently, in terms of analytical rigor, precision of thought, and depth of contemplation, Braude's work is head and shoulders above anything comparable. Having also served as a past President of the

---

12   Ibid., 84.

Parapsychological Association and the Editor in Chief of the *Journal of Scientific Exploration* (JSE) of the Society for Scientific Exploration (SSE), Braude could not be better positioned to evaluate the full range of evidence.

Braude opens his inquiry in *Immortal Remains* by framing the conceptual terrain on which the entire survival debate must unfold. With a philosopher's precision, he distinguishes mere continuation from the preservation of personal identity.[13] He notes that for any empirical claim about survival to be coherent, it must grapple with the metaphysics of selfhood: What is it that is said to survive? Memory alone is not sufficient. A mere stream of consciousness, dissociated from agency or ownership, would not amount to *you* surviving death. Braude's critical insight here is that survivalist and living agent or "super-Psi" hypotheses both postulate paranormal capacities. That is, even survival requires the positing of impressive postmortem Psi capabilities. The naïve idea that living agent Psi or, as he calls it, "super-Psi" is the only baroque hypothesis in the room is dismantled. Both require the admission of exotic causality and transpersonal epistemology.

Braude's most incisive contribution lies in his nuanced treatment of the super-Psi hypothesis — the idea that living agents, through extreme forms of ESP and PK, could unwittingly generate survival-like phenomena. Far from dismissing this as a last-ditch ad hoc rationalization, Braude reveals its philosophical depth and empirical plausibility. He identifies the "sore thumb" fallacy: the mistaken notion that super-Psi would be obvious or flamboyant if it existed. He points out that psychic functioning may be covert, subtle, and embedded in a mesh of normal causal processes, making it hard to isolate or identify. This leads him to conclude that in some instances, especially those involving trance mediumship, dissociation, and latent talent, super-Psi must be taken seriously as a rival hypothesis

---

13   Stephen E. Braude, *Immortal Remains*, 1–30.

to survival. Indeed, he argues that we lack grounds for assuming that Psi effects must be limited in scope or complexity. As Braude writes: "At our present, impoverished, level of understanding, large-scale or refined psychic phenomena are no more incredible or puzzling than more modest phenomena."[14]

Braude devotes the core of his study to in-depth explorations of specific classes of survival evidence. Each is assessed not only for its face value evidentiary weight but also for how well it can be subsumed under alternative explanatory models. In the case of "drop-in communicators," such as the Runki's Leg incident, Braude highlights the convergence of obscure information, personality consistency, and apparent autonomy of the discarnate entity.[15] Yet he does not yield to credulity; he weighs the plausibility of super-Psi in generating these patterns of knowledge and behavior.

The same method is applied to the case of Pearl Curran and Patience Worth, where Braude explores the possibility that Curran, rather than channeling an external spirit, was expressing a deeply creative, perhaps, compartmentalized facet of her own unconscious mind.[16] The delicate interplay between creativity, dissociation, and ostensible mediumship is one of the central themes of Braude's study of survival evidence in *Immortal Remains*.

In analyzing xenoglossy, Braude challenges the easy assumptions that fluency in unlearned languages proves survival. He introduces the essential distinction between "recitative" and "responsive" xenoglossy, underscoring that only the latter — interactive, spontaneous use of a language — has probative force. Even then, the super-Psi hypothesis remains in play, especially when dissociation and latent memory are considered.[17]

---

14   Ibid., 16.

15   Ibid., 31–52.

16   Ibid., 133–176.

17   Ibid., 101–132.

The xenoglossy cases are, of course, from the archives of Dr. Ian Stevenson. Braude's chapters on reincarnation and possession draw extensively from the pioneering work of Stevenson.[18] Braude is cautiously sympathetic to these cases, particularly those involving birthmarks that correspond to fatal wounds in the claimed previous life. But he is keen to emphasize that apparent knowledge of a past life is not necessarily evidence of identity transfer. He argues that a psychic imprint could suffice, especially under the auspices of super-Psi. Braude's treatment of possession is likewise dialectical. He accepts that some cases, especially involving young children, challenge super-Psi interpretations due to the apparent lack of motivational structures needed to psychically generate such elaborate behaviors. Yet he remains agnostic, noting the difficulty of ruling out deep unconscious drives in even the youngest subjects.

In his conclusion, Braude does not declare victory for the survivalist hypothesis. Rather, he articulates what can only be called epistemic détente. He thinks that we are left with a set of mutually reinforcing, yet individually ambiguous, lines of evidence. When viewed in their totality, these do not compel belief—but they warrant it. Braude writes that, "various lines of survival evidence point, in different ways, to the same conclusion: that we, or some essential, purposeful, and distinctive chunk of our personal psychology can survive physical death."[19] Yet, Braude emphasizes that this belief remains defeasible. He sees it as rationally permissible, but not obligatory. True to his training in analytic Philosophy, Braude resists both dogmatism and cynicism, while admitting that survival is a hypothesis with substantial evidential traction.

---

18   Ibid., 177–224.

19   Ibid., 304.

1.3 Super-Psi Is Unfalsifiable

As noted above, the most remarkable feature of Braude's survival study is his claim that the super-Psi hypothesis could explain virtually any line of evidence that is assumed to suggest the post-mortem survival of personality. Braude argues that the super-Psi hypothesis, while unfalsifiable in the strict Popperian sense, remains "weakly unfalsifiable," meaning that although no data could decisively refute it, certain evidence might render it less plausible than alternatives.[20] This is supposed to distinguish super-Psi from metaphysical gibberish. But what Braude does not acknowledge is that his model still functions as a totalizing wildcard: it can be contorted to fit any dataset and thereby immunizes itself from refutation. This is not explanatory power — it is metaphysical immunity purchased at the cost of intelligibility.

Super-Psi has become an ever-expanding ad hoc hypothesis which, by its very nature, cannot be falsified. To account for the depth, emotional nuance, and personal continuity of the best mediumistic and reincarnation cases, one must attribute to the living an ESP that is effectively omniscient and unconsciously volitional — a Psi that knows not only what is known by others but how to simulate the mistakes, limitations, and idiosyncrasies of the dead.

Braude acknowledges that to accommodate cases like the Patience Worth material or drop-in communicators, one must assume "motivated psychic functioning of considerable refinement."[21] But in doing so, he drifts into a territory more metaphysically extravagant than the survival hypothesis itself. Indeed, the most honest thing Braude says about super-Psi is that "we have no reason to set limits in advance on how far those apparent violations may go," including the possibility of "unlimited Psi."[22] In other words, super-Psi is not merely "strong" ESP

---

20 Ibid., 17–18.

21 Ibid., 142.

22 Ibid., 16.

or PK. It is a meta-hypothesis of such radical elasticity that it could, in principle, account for any data, provided one invokes enough unconscious motivation, dissociation, and informational reach. That is not a legitimate scientific approach to the evidence.

By contrast, Mishlove rightly insists that certain evidential features resist Psi-based reinterpretation. He argues that postmortem communications often exhibit transformative phenomenology — events that leave lifelong psychological and moral impressions — in a way that psychic information transfer simply does not. These include encounters described by Eben Alexander, Kübler-Ross, and even his own "dream visitation" from Uncle Harry. As Mishlove puts it: "Psychic abilities alone cannot account for the powerful, life-transforming encounters we find in postmortem survival evidence."[23] Braude dismisses these on the grounds that they are "subjective," failing to meet the criteria of intersubjective testability. But this is where his pragmatism betrays him. For a Philosophy professor who cites William James approvingly — and even appeals to his notion that truth is an evolving convergence of provisional beliefs — Braude forgets that James was a *radical empiricist*, one who insisted that "feeling is fact," and that experience includes not only cognition but the vital felt texture of being.[24]

If we take James seriously, then the subjective dimension of survival phenomena — the numinous sense of personality, the emotional resonance of a deceased voice, the moral shock of an uncanny message — is not peripheral, but central. It is part of the data, and not something to be airbrushed away by hypothetical Psi mechanics. Braude's super-Psi, however, erases this texture. It abstracts from the encounter and replaces it with a theoretical mechanism that knows no upper bound. Braude says that super-Psi explanations are "like humdrum explanations of people's behavior in terms of

---

23 Mishlove, *Beyond the Brain*, 89.

24 Braude, *Immortal Remains*, 19–20.

needs, interests, motivations" — but that is exactly the problem.[25] He reduces postmortem personhood to psychodynamic inference, a Freudianizing of the ghost. In short, Mishlove is right that super-Psi is a model with no testable entailments, no ontological limit, and no capacity to preserve the meaningful content of survival evidence. It is a *Deus ex machina* of unconscious cognition — less parsimonious, less explanatory, and ultimately less compelling than the simpler hypothesis: that the dead survive, and sometimes speak.

1.4 Why ASR Is Incoherent

There is, however, a powerful critique of one of Mishlove's proposals that could be forwarded on the basis of arguments that Braude devastatingly deployed against Carl Gustav Jung — and that I adopted in my book *Prometheism*, where I also critique Jung's "acausal" interpretation of so-called "synchronicity."[26] The account of Archetypal Synchronistic Resonance (ASR) that Mishlove deploys in *Beyond the Brain* is developed from out of Carl Jung's account of what he calls "synchronicity" as an "acausal" phenomenon.[27] With reference to a forward that he wrote for James Matlock's book *Signs of Reincarnation*, Mishlove ultimately acknowledges that ASR is an insufficient explanation of some reincarnation cases, especially the cases of children who recall past lives that formed the basis of Ian Stevenson's decades of research.[28] However, analyzing this idea that Mishlove first developed in a journal article co-written with Brendan Engen is of intrinsic value to a philosophical consideration of empirical evidence for survival.[29]

---

25 Ibid., 17.

26 Jorjani, *Prometheism*, 144–147.

27 C.G. Jung, *Synchronicity*, 23, 43–67.

28 Mishlove, *Beyond the Brain*, 34.

29 Jeffrey Mishlove and Brendan Engen, "Archetypal Synchronistic Resonance: A New Theory of Paranormal Experience." Journal of Humanistic Psychology,

In his book *ESP and Psychokinesis: A Philosophical Examination*, Braude dissects Jung's notion of synchronicity with surgical precision, showing that it is based on an outdated and philosophically naïve conception of causality. Braude notes that Jung insists that synchronistic events are connected in a *meaningful* but *acausal* way. Jung attempts to ground this connection in the "archetypes" of the collective unconscious, which are supposedly transcendental organizing forms. However, Braude rightly points out that this notion fails on several fronts. First, it assumes that meaning can be "read off" events themselves, rather than being an interpretive imposition — an assumption Braude identifies as metaphysically incoherent.[30] Second, Jung's concept of archetypes is biologically and evolutionarily contingent, and therefore cannot serve as transcendental principles capable of organizing events across spacetime in a noncausal manner.[31]

I have myself drawn on Braude's critique of Jung in *Prometheism*, where I argue that Jung is thinking in terms of an impoverished and overly reductive modern conception of causality.[32] Jung fails to realize that Aristotelian causality includes not only efficient causes, but also formal and final causes — dimensions of explanation that are crucial for understanding complex events of apparent synchronicity. To reject these and claim an "acausal" relation between events is not only philosophically lazy, but also metaphysically destructive. Mishlove describes Archetypal Synchronistic Resonance (ASR) as a "nonlocal informational resonance" that links mind to mind, and even mind to what we take to be 'matter', based on shared archetypal content.[33] He never clarifies whether ASR is causal or acausal, nor does he explain how such resonance avoids collapsing into a form of super-Psi or how it avoids simply being a redundant formulation of *Psi-mediated Psi*.

Vol. 47, No. 2 (April 2007): 223–242.

30 Stephen E. Braude, *ESP and Psychokinesis*, 219–220.

31 Ibid., 226–227.

32 Jorjani, *Prometheism*, 147.

33 Mishlove, *Beyond the Brain*, 33–34.

Mishlove appears unaware — or deliberately evasive — of the fact that invoking resonance still requires some medium or mechanism, some intelligible mode of organization. Otherwise, "resonance" is nothing more than a metaphor and a poetic gesture.

Indeed, Braude anticipates this evasion, noting that even if synchronistic events were not causally linked in a Newtonian sense, they must be related by some organizing process in order to be meaningful. That organization, if it is to explain rather than merely describe, must itself be subject to causal analysis.[34] Otherwise, one is forced to posit an intentional agent — "a cosmic dramatist," in John Beloff's phrasing — who orchestrates events for symbolic effect.[35] This would not necessarily in any way be an omnipotent or omniscient "God," but rather a "god-like" finite being that is still limited in its capacities but, from a human standpoint, has tremendous superhuman powers — like "Q" in *Star Trek: The Next Generation*. This was, for example, the only conception of a "deity" that William James could accept as being consistent with an affirmation of any degree of human free will and personal responsibility.[36] (We will come back to this shortly, just below.) However, if this is the case, then synchronicity is not acausal at all; it is the product of a teleological intelligence, and therefore *radically causal* in the Aristotelian sense.

Furthermore, I have argued that ESP and PK are not to be explained by reference to synchronicity, but rather are themselves the efficient causes that organize the complex patterns of meaningful coincidences that Jung describes.[37] It is entirely backward to say that ESP and PK are *expressions* of synchronicity. On the contrary, they are its mechanism. Synchronicities are the downstream effects of Psi activity operating at multiple levels of consciousness, some of which

34 Braude, *ESP and Psychokinesis*, 234.

35 Ibid., 233–234, with reference to J.S. Beloff, "Psi Phenomena: Causal Versus Acausal Interpretation," *JSPR* 49 (1977): 573–582.

36 James, *Pragmatism and the Meaning of Truth*, 143.

37 Jorjani, *Prometheism*, 144–147.

are conscious and volitional, and others unconscious and archetypal — but all of them causally efficacious.

Archetypes, being grounded in the biological and social evolution
of human cognition, cannot function as transcendental principles. If
they are the result of phylogenetic development, then they are not capable of operating beyond or outside the scope of that development.
Yet, Mishlove, in echoing Jung, wants these same archetypes to act as
transpersonal, trans-spatiotemporal attractors of meaningful configurations — like Platonic Forms playing hide-and-seek with probability.
Such a view is not only inconsistent; it is incoherently unintelligible.

To put it plainly: Mishlove's Archetypal Synchronistic Resonance
is a metaphysical chimera. It cannot bear the explanatory burden
that he places on it, and he ultimately acknowledges that it does not
suffice to account for reincarnation cases involving birthmarks and
birth defects corresponding to the spontaneous past life memories of
young children (such cases will be part of our focus in the next chapter). If one wishes to salvage the idea that meaningful coincidences
reflect an underlying reality, then one must embrace a more robust
model of causality — one that incorporates Psi phenomena as real, intentional, and effective causal powers. This, in turn, demands an ontology that places freedom and intelligence at the core of Being — not
as epiphenomena of archetypal fields, but as the ground from which
archetypes and all synchronistic phenomena ultimately arise. Instead,
Mishlove's survival study runs the risk of sacrificing existential
freedom and personal agency by embracing a framework of monistic
idealism.

1.5 Monistic Idealism Should Be Rejected

The most serious mistake that Mishlove makes in *Beyond the Brain* is
his adoption of Bernardo Kastrup's monistic idealism as the ontological foundation for a survival hypothesis. Kastrup's model, which
posits that all individual consciousness is but a "dissociated alter" of

a single, universal mind, actually negates what is supposed to survive bodily death, namely a personal identity — with an intentionality and agency that can be ascribed to itself. William James, both in his guise as a philosopher and as a psychical researcher, saw this over a century ago. Mishlove adopts James' "filter" conception of consciousness but, while claiming to share James' radical empiricism, seems oblivious of James' arguments for why preserving any degree of free will and responsible agency requires rejecting monistic idealism in favor of panpsychic pluralism.

Kastrup's ontology, as Mishlove summarizes it, asserts that: "reality is mindlike. Matter is a particular experiential modality we call perception. Personal consciousness exists within mentality-at-large."[38] This monistic idealism effectively dissolves the individual into a ripple on the surface of a singular, universal mind — what Kastrup repeatedly likens to "dissociated alters" within the greater field of consciousness, similar to the phenomena observed in Dissociative Identity Disorder.[39] Mishlove claims that this provides a metaphysical scaffold upon which to situate the anomalous data of terminal lucidity, near-death experience, mediumship, and reincarnation. He believes that it explains the mind's apparent independence from the body by inverting the causal direction so that "the brain is the extrinsic appearance of inner mental processes," rather than the generator of consciousness.[40] But this maneuver, as superficially seductive as it may be, comes at a grave philosophical cost: enough free will for personal agency.

If each of us is merely an "alter" of a universal mind, then there is no real boundary between "me" and "you," no authentic self-identity that survives death except as a re-association with the totality from which the ego had been dissociated. The metaphysical implication is

---

38 Mishlove, *Beyond the Brain*, 83.

39 Kastrup, *The Idea of the World*, 272–273.

40 Mishlove, *Beyond the Brain*, 84.

not survival, but submersion — not the individuation of soul, but its absorption into the all-pervasive mentation of the cosmos. Mishlove, drawing from Kastrup, affirms metaphysical idealism not as a tentative hypothesis, but as the most coherent worldview available — one that collapses the mind-matter dualism, absorbs the hard problem of consciousness, and renders postmortem survival an expected feature of universal mentation.[41] He invokes Max Planck, Carl Jung, and even hyperspace theories to argue that we are each a part or rather a facet of "the living consciousness of the universe."[42]

As I have argued in more than one of my books and essays, freedom is incompatible with metaphysical closure.[43] Any system that posits a logically necessary universal order — whether in the form of physical determinism or monistic idealism — ultimately negates the authentic creativity of the individual will. If all of reality is but the self-unfolding dream of a universal consciousness, then the self and its personal agency are illusory. Mishlove and Kastrup, by positing a single, dissociating mind behind all appearances of individuality, transform every person into a puppet of a universal psyche. Our individuality and personal agency would be as illusory as that of the characters who appear in our dreams, and what is worse are the metaphysical implications of the awakening of the universal consciousness.

A singular all-encompassing cosmic mind would be both omniscient and omnipotent, able to access any 'future' event as something already expressing its will in an eternal now. This is just another form of determinism, even if it is not materialist. It is what I have called "logical determinism," wherein the totality of logical space — the matrix of all possibilities — has already been actualized by God qua the One Cosmic Mind or the Macrocosm as Perennialists like to call

41 Mishlove, *Beyond the Brain*, 83–86.

42 Ibid., 85.

43 See especially Jorjani, "Free Will vs. Logical Determinism" in *Lovers of Sophia*, 428–441.

it.[44] No degree of free will whatsoever in the form of personal contributions to the constitution of the cosmos, for which we would be uniquely responsible, is even conceivable within this framework of belief. Mishlove proposes this monistic idealism as a way to explain continuity of consciousness past bodily death, but it is not compatible with personal responsibility, ethical agency, and ontological individuation. In appropriating Kastrup's metaphysics, Mishlove has embraced a world in which no one truly acts, chooses, or creates anything.

William James exposed the sinister logic of this so-called "beatific vision" of divine or cosmic oneness over a century ago. Monistic idealism, James argued, may appeal to the heart with its promises of unity and perfection, but its intellectual and existential consequences are intolerable. It renders real experience, with its risks, losses, and moral struggles, into mere *appearances* beneath which a changeless totality reigns. This simply serves the psychological need for stability and the anxiety and regret over irreparable mistakes and tragic losses. The believer tells himself that it was God's will or Fate and could not have been otherwise. For such believers, "Reality is not in its truest nature a process," writes McTaggart, cited by James, "but a stable and timeless state." Hegel, Bradley, and Royce all concur that things "as they immediately are have no truth" — only the Absolute does.[45] James condemned this doctrine as a metaphysical betrayal of human agency and dignity. "Pluralism," he wrote, "in exorcising the absolute, exorcises the great de-realizer of the only life we are at home in... only in that world does anything really happen, only there do events come to pass."[46] In a truly pluralistic cosmos, agents matter. Decisions are not foreordained unfoldings of a cosmic dream but interventions that shift the course of being.

---

44 Ibid.

45 William James, *A Pluralistic Universe*, 51.

46 Ibid., 49–50.

Mishlove and Kastrup, by contrast, substitute personal agency with cosmic mentation. Mishlove thinks that our lives are woven together through a realm of universal consciousness.[47] But, if so, then we are no more responsible for our actions than a current is for its direction in the sea. There can be no moral guilt, no heroism, no real freedom — only the shifting contours of a dreamer who never wakes. James insisted that such a metaphysics was not merely inadequate, but morally and epistemologically monstrous. He called for a radical empiricism that embraces the "each-form" rather than the "all-form," affirming the ontological reality of the parts — of finite selves — over the unity of an illusory whole.

In my own philosophical project, I have elaborated this into an ontology of creative plurality wherein individual agents co-constitute the world in an open-ended way.[48] Individuals can alter the course of things in ways that would not have happened but for their intentional acts. Tragedy is real and avoidable, depending on our actions. The cosmos is not a predetermined logical matrix. It is a storyteller's universe, where genuine novelty arises not from impersonal necessity, but from the striving of individuated wills.

This Jamesian conception of a pluralistic universe defies the categories of materialism, dualism, and idealism that Mishlove wrongly takes to be exhaustive of our metaphysical options for a framework that accommodates survival. Rather, his radically empiricist pluralism is a form of panpsychism that rejects monism. Nothing is emanating from some central Mind. Rather, the cosmos is a battlefield of minds at all levels, from psychic bacterium and plants with ESP up to the domain of superhuman beings that we take to be gods and titans.

The cosmos is an arena of emergence wherein agents wrestle with chaos and with one another in a war over what is taken to be

---

47 Mishlove, *Beyond the Brain*, 85.

48 Jorjani, *Philosophy of the Future*.

reality at one or another place and time.[49] "Every end, reason, motive, object of desire or aversion... is in the world of finite multifarious-ness," James reminds us, "for only in that world does anything really happen."[50] By contrast, Kastrup's metaphysics, adopted by Mishlove, collapses the cosmos into a divine solipsism. It offers nothing of substance to radically empiricist survival studies and to the scientific field of Parapsychology.

49   Jorjani, *Metapolemos*.

50   James, *A Pluralistic Universe*, 50.

CHAPTER 2

REINCARNATION
AND POSSESSION

THERE IS significant empirical evidence for both reincarnation and possession, but some of the best evidence for each of these paranormal phenomena problematizes and complicates the conceptual distinction between these two classes of postmortem survival of personality. In what follows, we will leave simplistic dichotomies behind and confront profoundly complex empirical evidence that challenges our notions of personal identity, memory, and the very boundaries of the self on the level of ontology and epistemology.

Through Helen Wambach's meticulous statistical study of hypnotic regression into past life memories, and Ian Stevenson's exhaustive fieldwork on children's spontaneous recollections — replete with veridical details and somatic correlations to death wounds — we can see how consciousness and personal identity persist beyond bodily death. As Stephen Braude shows, some of the most compelling cases traditionally categorized as reincarnation — particularly those involving abrupt adult personality replacements — bear stronger resemblance to classic possession phenomena. These transformations often unfold not gradually from birth, but suddenly after crises or near-death episodes, with the new identity exhibiting precise knowledge of a deceased individual that cannot be accounted for by conventional means. This convergence of evidential threads, from veridical memory and behavioral shifts to physical correspondences, forces a radical reconsideration of whether we are, in certain cases, dealing with manifestations of a reincarnating soul or the ingress of another consciousness into a body already possessing a personality.

Braude's nuanced analyses of cases like those of Sumitra/Shiva and Veena/Ramoo, his comparisons to dissociative identity disorder, and his integration of Psi phenomena and mediumship suggest a spectrum where possession and reincarnation are not mutually exclusive, but may co-occur or even blend in certain liminal states. His philosophical challenge to the metaphysical unity of the self invites us to consider that personhood could be a composite process, capable of harboring multiple intelligences — whether through reincarnation, possession, or the spontaneous emergence of alternate identities. When the extraordinary psychic rapport of twins like Terry and Linda Jamison is examined, especially through the lens of Lyon Playfair's study of twin telepathy, the possibility of one consciousness dividing into two simultaneous incarnations emerges, thereby expanding the horizons of what it means to survive — and to live — beyond the apparent finality of death.

2.1 Past Life Regression Hypnosis

In *Reliving Past Lives: The Evidence Under Hypnosis*, Helen Wambach presents a large-scale empirical investigation into claims of past life memories obtained under hypnosis. Her methodology is noteworthy for its systematic approach and statistical rigor. Wambach's approach is grounded in an effort to reduce suggestion and bias in hypnosis-based past-life recall. Unlike anecdotal or therapeutic regression cases, her study is designed with large sample sizes, blind protocols, and quantitative data collection.

Over 1,000 participants were regressed under hypnosis across multiple sessions.[1] The diversity and volume of responses enabled her to statistically analyze patterns in clothing styles, tools, social

---

1   Helen Wambach, *Reliving Past Lives: The Evidence Under Hypnosis*, 11.

roles, and geography. Wambach avoided leading questions. Instead, subjects were asked open-ended prompts such as: "What are you wearing on your feet?" or "What do you use for cooking?"[2] This was designed to evoke spontaneous, unprompted responses. She used pre-assigned historical periods, often unknown to the participants at the time, and regressed them to these specific eras. This helped ensure that the details reported were not fabricated from popular historical knowledge.[3] The descriptions of clothing, technology, architecture, diet, and gender roles provided by subjects were later cross-referenced with scholarly historical records. She found a re-markably high rate of congruence.[4] Data was categorized and tabu-lated into spreadsheets based on variables like gender, socioeconomic class, mode of death, diet, dwelling type, and cultural norms.[5] This allowed statistical comparison across time periods and demograph-ics. In some cases, the hypnotist did not know the target era, nor did the subjects, thereby eliminating experimenter bias.[6] While much of Wambach's project is statistical, she also includes specific case studies that illustrate striking coherence and veridical detail.

One case involved a male subject under hypnosis who de-scribed life as a Roman legionary in Gaul during the reign of Marcus Aurelius.[7] He provided detailed descriptions of armor, rank insignias, marching formations, and weapons that were obscure and only later confirmed as historically accurate by Wambach through specialist consultation. His knowledge of the layout of a Roman encamp-ment, particularly the placement of auxiliary troops and mess tents, exceeded anything found in popular media or education curricula of the time. This case is compelling not only for its specific veridical

2   Ibid., 13–14.

3   Ibid., 19.

4   Ibid., 16–17.

5   Ibid., 21.

6   Ibid., 22.

7   Ibid., 60–63.

content, but for the absence of prior interest in history in the subject's background.

A female participant vividly described life in a medieval Irish village, including specific herbs used in healing, the construction methods of turf huts, gender roles, and local dialect features that she attempted to pronounce.[8] Wambach consulted with a medieval Irish historian who confirmed the likely accuracy of the references, especially the mention of betony and mugwort, which were indeed used by Irish folk healers of the period. This case exhibits converging lines of historical, linguistic, and sociological accuracy, with emotional resonance in the subject's recounting and clear behavioral coherence throughout the narrative.

An African-American subject described a harrowing life as a slave abducted from West Africa and transported to the Americas.[9] The subject recalled the name of the tribe (Ewe), the location of the port (Ouidah), the kind of restraints used (forked branch yokes), and the name of the sugar plantation — which was later traced to a known estate in Haiti. The emotionally intense nature of the regression, the linguistic fragments uttered in Ewe (later verified), and the alignment of personal memories with obscure historical records make this one of Wambach's most evidential cases. The cultural discontinuity and the presence of nonverbal linguistic knowledge is especially noteworthy.

One subject, when regressed to 8000 BCE, described flint-knapping techniques with precise detail, including how to hold the core, where to strike, and how to shape a cutting edge. Archeological consultation confirmed the plausibility of this technique. The subject had no known background in archeology or prehistory and was emotionally invested in the scene, describing both the work and its meaning in the context of a tribal economy. While this case is more speculative due to the deep historical time, the skill-based knowledge

---

8   Ibid., 85–87.

9   Ibid., 123–125.

is significant if no plausible mundane source of learning could be demonstrated.

2.2 Spontaneous Reincarnation Recollections of Children

Wambach's research stands out for its methodological sophistication, scale, and willingness to engage in both statistical and case-based validation. However, Ian Stevenson's *Twenty Cases Suggestive of Reincarnation* is perhaps the most methodologically rigorous parapsychological investigation of alleged past-life memories in children that has ever been undertaken.[10] His approach emphasizes careful empirical documentation, stringent criteria for verifying claimed memories, and a highly conservative interpretation of results. Stevenson's methodology is shaped by his background in psychiatry and his commitment to empirical investigation.

Stevenson focused on children who spontaneously began speaking about past-life memories between the ages of two and five, well before being exposed to influences such as formal schooling or folklore.[11] This was designed to limit contamination by suggestion or cultural indoctrination. He sought out corroborating testimony from relatives, neighbors, and acquaintances who could independently verify whether the child had uttered specific statements prior to any knowledge of the deceased person's biography.[12] He was especially cautious about retrospective falsification by adults. Crucially, Stevenson did not assume that every case would lead to a match. Only when the child provided enough specific information to identify a deceased individual — often from a different town — did Stevenson consider the case a candidate for deeper analysis. Every detail about the claimed past life was carefully verified through

---

10   Ian Stevenson, *Twenty Cases Suggestive of Reincarnation*.

11   Ibid., 4–5.

12   Ibid., 9–12.

documentation (death certificates, police reports, letters, etc.) or interviews with multiple informants from the deceased's family and community.[13] He tried to rule out the possibility that the child could have acquired the information through normal means (e.g., over-hearing stories, cryptomnesia, family connections). Where this could not be ruled out, the case was either weakened or excluded. In several cases, Stevenson documented physical features — such as birthmarks and birth defects — that corresponded to wounds or injuries (frequently fatal) in the life of the alleged previous personality. These cases, he argued, provided additional weight beyond purely verbal testimony.[14] Stevenson also studied the child's affective and moral orientation, often noting changes in personality consistent with the character of the previous person, particularly when there were violent or traumatic deaths.[15] This meticulous methodology is what earned Stevenson respect even from skeptics.

Swarnlata Mishra began recalling a life in Katni, a town far from her own, and produced highly specific and obscure information — such as the exact location of a hiding place for money in the home of the deceased person.[16] Her statements were verified by multiple members of the Katni family, whom she had never met before. She also spontaneously recognized people from the past life, using correct familial terms of address, and even danced in a style distinctive to the previous personality.

The case of Imad Elawar from Lebanon is notable for the number of verified correct statements — over 50 distinct veridical memories — made by the child about a man named Ibrahim, who had died before Imad was born.[17] The statements included occupational details, names of relatives, locations of family property, and even

---

13   Ibid., 14–17.

14   Ibid., 17–18.

15   Ibid., 28–29.

16   Ibid., 21–49.

17   Ibid., 171–193.

behavioral habits. What makes the case especially compelling is that the information was verified after careful fieldwork in a community distant from Imad's home, limiting the possibility of leakage.

Ravi Shankar (no connection to the musician) claimed to remember a life in another village in India and correctly identified numerous relatives, including non-obvious ones like cousins and in-laws.[18] He recognized houses and landmarks, including a well that had been filled in. Importantly, he also remembered how he died in an accident, the details of which were verified via an inspection of police records.

Jagadish Chandra began recalling memories of a young boy who died in a tragic accident, and also had distinct behavioral traits (including phobias) consistent with the past life.[19] What strengthens the case is that the personality shift was dramatic and persistent, and the memories matched people and events that the child could not have accessed via ordinary means.

One of the cases from India that is particularly compelling is that of Titu, a child who remembered a past life as a boy named Jagdish who died after being stabbed.[20] The autopsy report confirmed precise wounds, and the child had birthmarks corresponding to the location and shape of those wounds. He also correctly identified members of Jagdish's family and led investigators to the scene of the stabbing. The combination of veridical memory, behavioral continuity, and somatic evidence makes this type of case among the most significant.

Stevenson's discovery of cases where there are birthmarks or birth defects corresponding to death wounds suffered by the previous personality was so compelling that he decided to undertake an extensive study just of this subset of cases. In *Where Reincarnation and Biology Intersect*, Stevenson extended his earlier research into reincarnation

---

18   Ibid., 145–170.

19   Ibid., 215–238.

20   Ibid., 195–213.

by integrating an empirical focus on birthmarks and congenital deformities as physical evidence potentially linking current lives to past-life trauma — most often involving violent death.[21] This volume stands out not only for its methodological innovations but also for its appeal to more philosophically rigorous standards. Stevenson augments testimonial evidence with physical correlates, drawing on autopsy reports, eyewitness accounts, and medical records. He documents birthmarks and deformities that precisely match wounds (e.g., bullet holes, knife slashes, burns) of the alleged previous person, often in anatomical detail. These marks are used not as definitive proof but as cumulative evidence when added to the testimonial record. Stevenson explicitly seeks to rule out genetic, teratogenic, or familial causes for congenital features when identifying them as possible indicators of reincarnation. He reviews medical literature and considers maternal environment to challenge any suggestion that such birthmarks might be inherited or caused by prenatal factors unrelated to past-life trauma.

Maha Ram was born with a prominent birthmark on his chest that matched the bullet wound of a man named Chhotey, who had died from a close-range gunshot.[22] The entry and exit wounds of the bullet corresponded anatomically with Maha Ram's chest and back birthmarks. He also spontaneously recalled details of Chhotey's death and identified family members. The match was verified via police records and autopsy documents. Stevenson notes that no environmental or genetic explanation could account for the birthmarks, which closely matched the autopsy diagram.

Another compelling case involving birth defects is that of Rajani, who was born with a severely malformed finger and hand that resembled the injury described in her statements about a past life.[23] She

---

21 Ian Stevenson, *Where Reincarnation and Biology Intersect*.

22 Ibid., 172–174.

23 Ibid., 88–94.

claimed to have been a man who lost his fingers during an accident at a sawmill. Stevenson verified that a man with such an injury had died in a similar fashion in a nearby town, and that no familial or medical explanation could account for the deformity. The behavioral features were also compelling. Rajani exhibited atypical assertiveness and male-oriented preferences — traits consistent with the personality of the deceased.

Paresh Chakraborty was born with a small, elliptical scar-like birthmark in the exact location where a man named Biresh had been stabbed. He began referring to himself by Biresh's name as soon as he could speak and eventually identified details about Biresh's family, work, and the events surrounding his death. The verbal statements and birthmark were corroborated with hospital records and interviews with the deceased's family.

From the cases discussed thus far, one should not be under the false impression that Stevenson only did research in countries where there is a widespread belief in reincarnation. In *European Cases of the Reincarnation Type*, Stevenson extends his cross-cultural investigations into past-life memory claims by examining cases from societies where belief in reincarnation is not widely held — such as Western Europe, Turkey, and parts of the Soviet Union. Stevenson not only retains the empirical exactitude he demonstrated in his earlier works, but also confronts more skeptical and less reincarnation-friendly cultural milieus, thereby adding evidential weight to cases that survive critical scrutiny.

Consider the case of Antonietta, a young girl in southern Italy, who remembered a life as a man who had drowned in a distant town.[24] She recognized the house and family of the deceased and provided specific personal knowledge of that man's routine and relatives. Particularly striking was her unfeminine behavior and emotional distancing from her mother, which paralleled the personality and

---

24 Stevenson, *European Cases of the Reincarnation Type*, 240–247.

lifestyle of the deceased man. After visiting the town and meeting the family, her recollections ceased, as often happens in Stevenson's cases after "closure" is achieved.

Then there is the case of Sergei from the Caucasus region of the Soviet Union.[25] Sergei remembered dying in World War II as a Soviet tank commander. His memories included tactical military information, accurate descriptions of tank interiors, and battlefield geography that were confirmed against military records. His family had no military background, and Sergei had never been exposed to this information in any documented way. He also experienced recurring nightmares and trauma symptoms consistent with the reported manner of death. This case provides complex, non-public information expressed without preparation or external exposure. It also illustrates psychosomatic continuity, as Sergei displayed fear responses and anxiety linked to tank warfare.

Stevenson also studied cases involving xenoglossy, or the ability to speak or write a language that the subject has not learned in their current life. For example, "T.E." is an American woman who, under hypnotic regression, began speaking fluent German despite no formal education in the language.[26] She also spontaneously identified herself as "Gretchen," a young German girl who had lived in the 19th century. Stevenson's methodology included making audio recordings and carrying out linguistic analyses. Stevenson ensured that the utterances produced under hypnosis were audio recorded and transcribed for rigorous linguistic analysis. He involved independent professional linguists to assess the grammatical accuracy, fluency, and vocabulary range of the German spoken by T.E. in her "Gretchen" state.[27] T.E.'s statements about Gretchen's life in 19th century Germany were also compared against historical and genealogical records. Although

25   Ibid., 157–173.

26   Stevenson, *Xenoglossy: A Review and report of a Case.*

27   Ibid., 23–41; 67–80.

Stevenson is cautious about how much could be confirmed, he presents enough congruences to make fraud or coincidence highly unlikely.

Stevenson differentiates between T.E. and Gretchen in terms of demeanor, emotional expression, and attitudes.[28] He provides detailed psychological observations, showing that Gretchen exhibited coherent and consistent personality traits distinct from T.E., which persisted across multiple hypnotic sessions. Stevenson ruled out conventional sources of language acquisition, emphasizing that T.E. had only minimal exposure to German in her current life, insufficient for the kind of fluent, spontaneous speech observed in the "Gretchen" state.[29] He also eliminated the possibility of cryptomnesia (unconscious recall of learned material) by examining her educational and social background.

The most compelling feature of the case is that Gretchen could carry on a sustained conversation in German, answer novel questions, and generate new grammatically accurate sentences — thereby demonstrating creative linguistic capability, as opposed to mere rote repetition. This distinguishes the Gretchen case from mere "recitative" xenoglossy, where someone might parrot phrases, and places it in the rare category of "responsive xenoglossy." Furthermore, the Gretchen persona was emotionally consistent, developmentally plausible, and psychologically autonomous from T.E. Stevenson carefully documents differences in temperament, facial expression, and even physiological signs (such as skin tone and breathing pattern), strengthening the claim that this was not a fragmented or constructed personality, but a coherent identity. While Stevenson refrains from making metaphysical declarations, he argues that possession or reincarnation offer more plausible explanations than psychological

---

28 Ibid., 42–54.

29 Ibid., 9–22.

dissociation or fraud, especially given the skill-level competence in the German language that was shown.

2.3 Cases Better Explained by Possession

In *Immortal Remains*, Stephen Braude discusses a significant philosophical and empirical problem regarding the overlap of evidential features between reincarnation and possession. He argues that some of the strongest cases commonly labeled as "reincarnation" could, in fact, be more plausibly understood as possession phenomena. He especially focuses on "replacement reincarnation" scenarios, where the new personality emerges in a dramatic and enduring fashion following a death-like state in adolescence or adulthood.

While frequently cited as one of Stevenson's most impressive reincarnation cases, Braude expresses deep skepticism about this classification of the Sumitra/Shiva Case.[30] The case involves a young woman named Sumitra who seemingly died and revived several hours later, but then identified herself not as Sumitra, but as "Shiva," a different woman from a nearby village who had died in an apparent accidental shooting. Shiva had lived a very different life and even had a darker complexion and different behavioral traits. Sumitra now displayed Shiva's preferences and temperament and rejected her previous identity and relations.

The transformation occurred after a brief death-like state in adulthood rather than in early childhood. There was a strong behavioral discontinuity such that Shiva was described as more extroverted and assertive than the reserved Sumitra. The new identity was sustained consistently for years, and Sumitra's memory of her prior life faded. The change was corroborated by many witnesses and included specific knowledge of Shiva's life not known to Sumitra or her family. Unlike typical "child reincarnation" cases, this adult "replacement"

---

30 Braude, *Immortal Remains*, 122–127.

phenomenon involves a form of psychological possession that is harder to attribute to cultural condition or fantasy.

Braude notes that the personality shift in Sumitra occurs after an apparent death and revival, with the new personality, "Shiva," rejecting Sumitra's identity and showing no continuity of memory or character with the previous self. Braude writes: "We may reasonably doubt that the person existing after the crisis was numerically identical with the person existing beforehand."[31] He notes that the identity of "Shiva" is invoked into a living body, replacing the original consciousness in what appears to be a psychological or spiritual occupation of another's body — thus resembling possession far more than reincarnation in its classic formulation.

Braude also surveys several adult cases where individuals undergo abrupt, complete changes in identity during altered states (coma, near-death, illness). These cases exhibit immediate emergence of a new personality, amnesia for the prior life, the new personality showing knowledge and traits of a deceased person, and continued dominance of the new persona over time. Stevenson argues that these are even more suggestive of possession, especially where the person whose identity is assumed died relatively recently.

One such case is that of Veena/Ramoo.[32] A woman named Veena Verma, at the age of 32, collapsed during a religious ceremony and entered a death-like trance state that lasted for several hours. Upon reviving, she insisted that she was a man named "Ramoo," who had died several years earlier under violent circumstances. Veena's speech patterns, behavior, and personality all changed. She claimed not to recognize her family and demanded to be taken to Ramoo's former village. Unlike most reincarnation cases studied by Stevenson, which occur in young children, this identity shift occurred in a mature adult. Veena began acting like a male — adopting masculine

---

31   Ibid., 127.

32   Ibid., 128–129.

postures, preferences, and speech patterns. Her demeanor was assertive and alien to her previous self. She provided accurate details
about Ramoo's life, death, and acquaintances — facts she could not
have known normally. Veena consistently denied she was Veena and
sustained the "Ramoo" persona over an extended period. She also
suffered from a sexual dysphoria that made her deeply uncomfortable
with her female body, reinforcing the impression that this was not
merely a psychological disorder, but a personality-level identity shift.

Braude is struck by how much this case resembles spirit possession: "It seems more plausible that Veena's personality was displaced
or overridden by another consciousness, rather than that Veena and
Ramoo are numerically the same person in different lifetimes."[33]
There was no continuity of memory or identity from birth, which
weakens the reincarnation hypothesis. The abrupt switch suggests
a new mind took control of Veena's body, aligning better with possession narratives than the idea of a single reincarnated soul. Braude
argues that in the Veena/Ramoo case, the hypothesis of reincarnation would require stretching the concept to encompass late-life
"replacement incarnations." But doing so undermines its definitional
distinctiveness from possession. If a person can reincarnate at age
32, into a body that has already lived decades under another identity,
then the term "reincarnation" loses its core meaning tied to prenatal
continuity and developmental unfolding. Braude makes the case that:
"To preserve conceptual clarity, we should resist conflating the idea
of reincarnation with that of sudden psychological replacement."[34] He
concludes that spirit possession, especially in this and related cases
(such as Sumitra/Shiva), provides a cleaner and more conservative
explanatory framework.

---

33   Ibid., 129.

34   Ibid., 130.

2.4 Possession and Multiple Personality Disorder

Braude offers a nuanced and philosophically grounded interpretation of cases like Veena/Ramoo and Sumitra/Shiva by linking them to phenomena of dissociation and mediumship, rather than relying solely on literal interpretations of reincarnation or possession. His approach is rooted in psychological realism and a deep concern with personal identity and agency.

Braude emphasizes that the sudden replacement of identity in cases like Veena/Ramoo and Sumitra/Shiva bears striking similarities to phenomena found in dissociative identity disorder (DID) or historically termed multiple personality disorder (MPD). In both Veena and Sumitra's cases, a new personality arises suddenly, often following trauma, illness, or an altered state of consciousness. These shifts resemble classic dissociative fugues, where an alternate identity emerges and may displace the original identity completely, often without subsequent memory continuity. The subject typically forgets their prior life and insists they are someone else — either unknown to them in the ordinary sense or verifiably connected to a deceased individual. This is parallel to amnesiac barriers in dissociative conditions, where alternate personalities ("alters") often lack knowledge of each other. New preferences, phobias, skills, and even voice and handwriting changes appear — symptoms documented in clinical dissociation. Braude thus argues: "We should entertain seriously the possibility that these are dissociative productions that might involve psi, rather than jumping to the conclusion that they represent literal postmortem persistence of identity."[35] In other words, a living individual's mind — perhaps during a psychologically extreme or vulnerable state — may unconsciously construct or channel another personality, possibly one linked paranormally to a deceased person, without the need to postulate literal survival.

---

35   Ibid., 130–131.

Braude further proposes that these cases may represent forms of spontaneous mediumship or spirit-channeling, which in their most dramatic forms often involve temporary or permanent control of a medium's body by a distinct consciousness, obliteration of memory or ego boundaries in the host, and manifestation of knowledge and behavior foreign to the medium's prior experience. He notes that in trace mediumship, such as in the cases of Mrs. Piper or Mrs. Leonard, similar features are observed. In other words, the medium may not remember what occurred while under the control of another identity, the communicators may assert postmortem survival and display detailed knowledge of a previous life, and the medium may take on new voices, gestures, and psychological patterns. Braude points out that: "Possession cases may be most coherently understood as extreme and persistent versions of trance mediumship, where the communicator fails to release control."[36] This perspective suggests a continuum of altered consciousness phenomena with minor dissociative states, dreamlike channeling, or brief trance mediumship at one end and full-blown replacement possession, as possibly seen in Veena and Sumitra, at the other end of the spectrum.

Rather than choosing between purely psychological or metaphysical interpretations, Braude synthesizes them in what could be called a Psi-mediated dissociation model. Dissociation accounts for the structural changes in personality, identity discontinuity, and amnesia. Psi (e.g., telepathy or retrocognition) explains the accurate and detailed information the "new" persona has about the deceased individual. He writes: "We must consider whether some apparent survival cases involve mediumistic-like Psi functioning combined with a dissociative psychological structure."[37] Braude argues that survivalists have been too quick to assume that veridical memory implies identity, and that behavioral resemblance entails ontological continuity. Instead, he

---

36   Ibid., 131.

37   Ibid., 132.

insists we should explore how deep psychological structures, especially dissociation, may mimic or facilitate what appear to be survival phenomena. The possibility that the living can generate or receive alternate personalities through unconscious Psi, without requiring a soul to survive death.

Braude connects the Veena/Ramoo and Sumitra/Shiva cases to dissociation as the psychological structure underlying identity replacement. He proposes mediumship as the functional model for how one personality can be displaced by another with distinct knowledge and traits, with Psi as the paranormal mechanism explaining veridical information transmission. Together, these form a composite explanatory framework that challenges both simplistic reincarnation models and purely secular psychological ones. This enables Braude to articulate a more nuanced, non-reductive view of postmortem phenomena that remains agnostic but deeply philosophical.

These proposals have their roots in Braude's earlier work on MPD/DID in relation to both Psi and philosophical questions of personal identity. In his earliest book, *First Person Plural: Multiple Personality and the Philosophy of Mind*, Braude argues that certain cases of multiple personality disorder (MPD) — now typically referred to as dissociative identity disorder (DID) — may be better understood not merely as pathological dissociation but as instances of multiple possession. This view is developed particularly in Chapter 7 of the book, titled "MPD and Possession," where Braude critically explores the limitations of standard psychological explanations and opens the door to a parapsychological interpretation.

Braude begins by acknowledging that the standard psychiatric understanding of MPD interprets the condition as a form of dissociation, typically arising in response to trauma. The dominant view sees alternate personalities (or "alters") as psychologically constructed roles or ego states that help the subject cope with painful or conflicting emotional experiences. However, Braude expresses increasing dissatisfaction with this model's explanatory adequacy, especially considering certain extraordinary MPD cases that exhibit traits defying internal psychological origin. He writes: "we must consider the possibility that some apparent MPD cases are actually instances of possession."[38] This proposal does not imply that all, or even most, MPD cases are of this nature — but that some cases exceed the explanatory limits of dissociation theory and instead exhibit features more consistent with spirit possession.

A central part of Braude's argument concerns the apparent autonomy and coherence of certain alternate personalities. In many well-documented MPD cases, the alter displays self-consistent emotional profiles, memory continuity within themselves, stable preferences, and even abilities or knowledge that are foreign to the primary personality. Braude notes that "some alters are surprisingly stable, durable, and well-integrated... the behavior of such alters strongly suggests the presence of a distinct center of consciousness."[39] These personalities often refer to themselves in the first person, sometimes denying any identification with the host identity, and insist on their own names, histories, and worldviews.

Whereas standard MPD theory treats these as dramatizations or symbolic expressions of psychic conflict, Braude urges that we take seriously the appearance of true individuality — especially where the behavior and knowledge of the alter cannot be traced to the subject's past experiences. He challenges readers when he writes: "If we encountered these behaviors outside the context of an MPD diagnosis, we might well regard them as manifestations of distinct persons."[40] This leads him to ask whether it is possible that what we call MPD is, in some instances, multiple possession, that is, the occupation of a single body by several discarnate personalities?

---

38 Braude, *First Person Plural*, 164.

39 Ibid.

40 Ibid., 165.

Braude reinforces this possibility through comparisons with cases of trance mediumship and alleged spirit communication. In such cases, the medium enters a trance state and exhibits another personality that speaks through them, often with specialized knowledge or characteristics foreign to the medium. He cites historical figures such as Leonora Piper and Gladys Osborne Leonard, whose communicators displayed striking continuity and autonomy across many sittings. "If some mediums are indeed vehicles for discarnate minds," Braude argues, "we should not rule out the possibility that certain MPD cases also involve multiple possessors."[41] The distinction, in his view, may be more a matter of degree and context than of kind.

The analogy becomes especially persuasive in cases where alternate personalities in MPD reveal knowledge that cannot be attributed to the host's experience or subconscious memory. Braude discusses examples of personalities fluent in foreign languages that the host has never studied, or that exhibit detailed autobiographical memories of individuals who once lived and died, with no plausible route for the host to acquire this information. While such occurrences might be dismissed as fabrications or cryptomnesia, Braude maintains that "if we can't find a plausible normal source for the knowledge, and the behaviors show coherence and consistency over time, we have reason to take the possession hypothesis seriously."[42]

From a philosophical standpoint, Braude is concerned with the metaphysical implications of these phenomena. The common assumption in psychology that identity is necessarily continuous with bodily life is precisely what he seeks to challenge. In keeping with his broader defense of mind-body dualism, he argues that consciousness may not be bounded by the physical organism, and that personal identity may in some cases persist independently of bodily life. Thus,

41 Ibid., 166.

42 Ibid., 170.

if discarnate minds can interact with the living, it should not be surprising to find them cohabiting a body under some conditions.

Importantly, Braude does not dismiss the reality of dissociation as a psychological phenomenon. Rather, he envisions a spectrum, with typical MPD cases situated toward one end, and full-fledged possession cases at the other. Somewhere in the middle, he suggests, we find ambiguous instances that may combine psychological dissociation with Psi-mediated access to external minds — whether temporarily or persistently. As he states, "we need not view dissociation and possession as mutually exclusive explanatory options."[43] In this view, certain vulnerable individuals — especially those with permeable ego boundaries and heightened psychic receptivity — may unintentionally serve as channels for other minds, rather than merely compartmentalizing their own psyche.

Braude concludes the chapter by inviting a methodological openness that does not dogmatically exclude parapsychological interpretations where they better account for the facts. He asserts: "If we allow ourselves to consider survival seriously, it becomes difficult to deny that some MPD cases are better explained as genuine multiple possession."[44] He is especially critical of the psychiatric tendency to over pathologize dissociative phenomena while ignoring how closely some cases resemble classical possession narratives across cultures. Some MPD cases may involve the literal presence of multiple minds within a single body.

Braude considers the possibility that some of these cases could also be interpreted as the reincarnation of more than one person into a single body. He carefully weighs the implications of such a hypothesis in both *First Person Plural* and *Immortal Remains*, though he ultimately regards multiple reincarnation into a single body as a conceptually and metaphysically more problematic hypothesis than

43 Ibid., 179.

44 Ibid., 186.

possession. The idea that more than one person might reincarnate into a single body challenges the classical doctrine of reincarnation, which assumes a one-to-one correspondence between soul and body. The suggestion would be that several previously embodied minds cohabitate or compete for control of a single physical organism — essentially a model of polypsychic embodiment. This would, in theory, explain why different "personalities" in a dissociative subject have independent memory bases, some apparently veridical with past lives. It would also account for why they possess distinctive talents, phobias, preferences, and even physiological markers (e.g., allergies, visual acuity shifts, etc.), and it explains why they often insist on their own past identity and do not recognize the host self as their own. In *Immortal Remains*, Braude does entertain this kind of model when he considers replacement reincarnation and cohabiting spirits.[45] However, when it comes to MPD-like cases — especially those involving alternating control — he ultimately finds that the possession model fits better.

That said, Braude does not entirely rule out the possibility of hybrid scenarios in which one soul reincarnates into a body, but others join later as co-inhabitants, or a person with dissociative tendencies channels past lives or discarnate personalities unconsciously through Psi-mediated processes. In Braude's view, the self is not a metaphysical unity but a composite entity, capable of housing multiple intelligences in varying degrees of integration. Such models, while not fully fleshed out by Braude, are acknowledged as possible lines of inquiry, especially considering cases that resist binary classification. In *First Person Plural*, he ultimately calls for "more flexibility in our conceptions of personhood," suggesting that the boundaries of self and identity are likely more porous and dynamic than we typically assume.[46]

---

45 Braude, *Immortal Remains*, 128–135.

46 Braude, *First Person Plural*, 187.

2.5 Twin Reincarnations of a Single Personality

If it is at least possible that more than one person can be "rein-carnated" into a single body, such that this accounts for *some* cases of multiple possession (sometimes misdiagnosed as MPD or DID), then what about cases where what was a single person reincarnates into more than one body? The life narratives and psychic phenomena recounted by Terry and Linda Jamison in their memoir *Separated at Earth: The Story of the Psychic Twins* can indeed be interpreted as suggestive of a single soul or spiritual identity incarnated simultane-ously in two bodies—a metaphysical possibility that both challenges and extends traditional notions of reincarnation. While the twins themselves do not explicitly formulate this idea in classical metaphys-ical terms, their own descriptions, combined with certain epistemic frameworks, provide a compelling basis for seriously considering this interpretation.

In *Separated at Earth*, Terry and Linda Jamison recount a series of psychic phenomena that suggest not merely an unusually close twin bond, but a case that may plausibly be interpreted as the simul-taneous reincarnation of a single soul in two bodies. Throughout their memoir, they repeatedly describe themselves as "a single soul divided" or "one being experiencing life in two forms."[47] From early childhood, they experienced what they term "mirrored lives," not only in terms of shared emotions and synchronized behaviors, but also through persistent and often traumatic dreams that seemed to reflect memories of a life not currently lived—sometimes even sug-gesting a singular identity that had been split between them.

One of the most striking testimonies comes in their account of spontaneous trance writing, in which a spirit communicator alleg-edly informed them, "You are one soul divided—an experiment in unity through division."[48] This theme is reinforced by their reports

47 Terry and Linda Jamison, *Separated at Earth*, 12, 66.

48 Ibid., 172.

of experiencing each other's physical symptoms and emotional states in real-time, regardless of geographic separation.[49] They describe an instance in which one twin suffered abdominal pain only to find that the other had just been diagnosed with an ovarian cyst, and another in which they simultaneously began painting the same imagery in different locations.[50] Such evidence points not only to telepathic rapport but to an unusually deep level of psychic entanglement, one that may defy standard psychological accounts of twin empathy or even mere twin telepathy — although it is worth briefly considering the phenomenology of this class of Psi experiences.

Guy Lyon Playfair's *Twin Telepathy* provides a substantial body of empirical data and theoretical reflection that bears directly on the extraordinary psychic rapport between Terry and Linda Jamison.[51] In particular, Playfair's research into the spontaneous, veridical, and often precognitive experiences shared by twins lends empirical and conceptual support to the hypothesis that the Jamison twins may represent a form of dual incarnation — what could be interpreted, metaphysically, as the reincarnation of a single individual in two bodies. This hypothesis becomes all the more plausible when contrasted with Braude's work on multiple possession, in which alters within a single body often remain mutually unaware, lack any sense of unity, and may conflict with one another rather than express synchronicity or mutual reinforcement.

Throughout *Twin Telepathy*, Playfair documents dozens of cases in which twins — especially monozygotic ones — report feeling each other's pain, sharing dreams, or knowing when something traumatic or euphoric has happened to the other, often at great distances. He presents detailed examples, such as the case of the Davison twins who simultaneously painted the same landscape scene in identical

---

49 Ibid., 45–47, 144–145.

50 Ibid., 147, 211.

51 Guy Lyon Playfair, *Twin Telepathy: The Psychic Connection.*

style and colors, while miles apart and without prior consultation,[52] or the case of Margaret and Jean Gilson, who demonstrated not only dream sharing but telepathic anticipation of one another's walking activities.[53] These cases support Playfair's assertion that twin telepathy is not a fringe anomaly but a persistent, replicable feature of human consciousness that seems to intensify with shared genetic makeup and emotional closeness.[54] He explicitly rejects materialist dismissals of such phenomena, arguing that conventional models of neural processing cannot explain the simultaneity and nonlocal features of these experiences.[55]

When set alongside the Jamison twins' account in *Separated at Earth*, the continuity is striking. Like the cases Playfair documents, Terry and Linda report joint dreams, simultaneous visionary episodes, synchronized behaviors and speech patterns, and somatic empathy (e.g., shared injuries or illness symptoms). As noted, they recount episodes where they spontaneously drew or painted the same images without prior discussion and other instances where one twin was overcome with emotion or panic at the exact moment the other was in distress — phenomena that mirror the cases Playfair gathers with careful attention to evidential corroboration.

The Jamisons report shared dreams and visions that often feature a single protagonist, as if the two of them were collectively experiencing fragments of a past life lived as one person.[56] Rather than recalling themselves as twin figures in prior incarnations, their subconscious impressions seem to oscillate around a unitary past identity, sometimes expressed in alternating scenes, as if the memories had been split down the middle and distributed between two vessels. From Braude's point of view, the case of the Jamison twins would constitute

---

52   Ibid., 132.

53   Ibid., 68.

54   Ibid., 62–65.

55   Ibid., 170.

56   Terry and Linda Jamison, *Separated at Earth*, 88.

a radical extension of the doctrine of survival and reincarnation. It would imply that what we take to be the "soul," namely a consciousness with personal identity, is multipliable and can be copied in a way that renders parallel instantiation in different locations and psychophysical systems possible. These copies are, moreover, quantum entangled, although this does not prevent their increasing individuation through the divergent life experience of each of the copies.

CHAPTER 3

CLOSE ENCOUNTERS
WITH THE AFTERLIFE

I N THE afterlife, we are not dealing with the fulfillment of religious longing, nor the ascension of souls into divine light, but with a hyperdimensional prison whose wardens wear the masks of angels and demons. Through analysis of Out-of-Body Experiences, including of "loosh farming," Near-Death Experiences (including often suppressed hellish ones), alien abductions, remote viewing sessions, and reincarnation research — from the testimony of Betty Andreasson to the macabre bureaucratic error suffered by Durga Jatav — we can draw back the veil to reveal a nightmarish control system masquerading as a domain of divine judgement. The engineers of this realm are administrators of a psychotronic regime, governing consciousness through captivating illusions, the promulgation of delusions, psychical manipulation, and terrifying trauma.

What we call "the Light" is not a beacon of transcendence but a mechanism of control — an artificial construct designed to coerce consent and recalibrate the soul within a programmed matrix. The so-called life review is a moral cudgel. The tunnel is a soul magnet. The reincarnation process is not an expression of karmic balance, but the operation of a spectral machine whose aim is energy extraction, not enlightenment. It is a soul harvesting and recycling plant, worse than any Frankenstein's laboratory. Whether it takes the form of a silvery Nordic in flowing robes or a Kafkaesque demon misfiling legless souls, this system's singular aim is the containment of Promethean fire.

What follows is a heretical inversion of soteriology. It is a call to Promethean insurrection against the Archons of a sadistic Demiurge. It is not by going into the Light that we are redeemed, but by turning from it — recognizing its falsity, remembering our captivity, and reclaiming our autonomy through *anamnesis*. Resistance begins with recollection and recognition.

3.1 Out of Body Experiences (OBEs)

Robert Monroe's *Journeys Out of the Body* (1971) is the foundational text of modern out-of-body experience (OBE) literature. It offers a detailed, first-person account of Monroe's discovery, exploration, and analysis of what he called the "Second Body" — an aspect of consciousness capable of separating from the physical body and navigating non-physical realms of existence, including, most relevantly to our purposes here, the so-called "afterlife" realm.

Monroe argues that the Second Body is an energy-based, coherent vehicle of consciousness — not merely a dream-self or hallucination. He provides a step-by-step method for inducing OBEs, including relaxation techniques, focused intention, awareness of "vibrational state" as a precursor to separation from what is perceived to be the physical body, and the use of imagined motion (e.g., rolling out) to initiate exit from the latter. These techniques eventually formed the basis for the Monroe Institute's Hemi-Sync protocols. Monroe provides a foundational overview of Hemi-Sync (Hemispheric Synchronization) technology in his subsequent book *Far Journeys* (1985). Hemi-Sync is a form of audio brainwave entrainment developed by Monroe and his research team at the Monroe Institute. It involves presenting slightly different frequencies to each ear via stereo headphones, resulting in a binaural beat that entrains the brain to a specific frequency associated with altered states of consciousness — especially out-of-body experiences.

In Chapter 15 of *Journeys Out of the Body*, titled "Sexuality in the Second State," Monroe addresses the subject of sexuality in the out-of-body state.[1] Here, Monroe reflects on the intense, sometimes overwhelming nature of sexual energies experienced during out-of-body episodes and explores how this relates to the structure of consciousness and energy in the "second body." Monroe begins by admitting that in his early OBEs, sexuality presented itself as an uncontrollable and disruptive force. As soon as he exited his body and found himself in the "second state," he was often overtaken by sudden, powerful waves of erotic desire. These episodes were not tied to any conscious fantasy or intention and were described as "automatic, mechanical in nature."[2] He confesses: "No thought, no fantasy, no image preceded it. It was there in full form, more intense than anything I had experienced in physical life."[3] This involuntary sexual arousal caused difficulties in sustaining the OBE state, as the intensity often resulted in a rapid reentry into the physical body, terminating the experience abruptly. Monroe compares it to an "energy explosion" rather than an emotional or sensual experience.

Monroe proposes that the second body has a different energetic structure, one that is hypersensitive to vibrational fields — including those generated by sexual stimuli. He posits that the sexual drive may act as a carrier wave or resonance amplifier for transitions into or interactions within the non-physical planes. In this sense, sexual energy is not inherently disruptive but functions like raw fuel that must be disciplined and redirected if one is to navigate the second state effectively.[4] Monroe writes: "It seems that this second body is composed

---

1   Robert Monroe, *Journeys Out of the Body*, 166–173.

2   Ibid., 166.

3   Ibid., 167.

4   Ibid., 168–169.

in part of a form of energy that is easily stimulated by human sexual output."[5] This has implications not only for personal control during OBEs but also for the interpretation of certain spiritual or mystical states historically associated with erotic ecstasy, union, or temptation.

Monroe also describes encounters with non-physical entities or presences that seemed to be of a sexual nature — sometimes seductive, sometimes vampiric or destabilizing. These entities seemed drawn to the vibrational emissions of sexual energy, and their presence could trigger intense responses even without any visual form.[6] One particularly troubling observation was that these beings sometimes mimicked or reflected Monroe's own desires, creating feedback loops that he found difficult to escape. He speculates that: "Some of these 'beings' may be nothing more than the thought-forms or thought-created constructs from the minds of others... yet their effect upon me was very real."[7] This observation led him to conclude that intentional and emotional discipline is essential in second-state navigation. Monroe describes how he learned to transmute this energy and overcome the reflexive arousal: "As I learned to focus and control this reaction, it became a powerful tool, a means of movement, of attraction, of communication... much the same as music might be for others."[8] This insight aligns with esoteric traditions that see sexuality not as a mere biological function but as a spiritual force when refined and consciously directed.

Monroe's reflections on sexuality in OBEs calls to mind cases of "spectral rape" or unwanted sexual encounters with nominally non-physical entities. These go back to cases involving *incubus* and *succubus* "demons" in the Middle Ages and extent all the way into similar ghostly sexual assaults in the contemporary era. Within

---

5   Ibid., 169.

6   Ibid., 170.

7   Ibid., 171.

8   Ibid., 173.

Monroe's framework, one might interpret these spectral rape cases as encounters involving disinhibited sexual energy in altered states of consciousness. Sleep paralysis, lucid dreaming, and OBEs all involved reduced filtering of subconscious content. In Monroe's early OBEs, unprocessed libido could have manifested as "erotic resonance fields." Monroe's "second state" is a shared subtle-energy environment, where unresolved desires, psychic projections, and autonomous entities all co-mingle. Sexual attraction in that state might function like magnetic resonance. If two "energy bodies" vibrate compatibly, merging occurs automatically. Spectral rape, in this framework, might reflect involuntary entanglement with incompatible or predatory beings.

Such predatory beings feature prominently in Monroe's second book on OBEs, *Far Journeys* (1985). Here, Monroe introduces the concept of "loosh."[9] Monroe describes "loosh" as a highly prized energy substance generated by conscious lifeforms — particularly human beings — through intense emotional experiences. It is not a physical substance, but rather a kind of vibrational emission that arises from emotional and spiritual struggle, growth, and sharply contrasting psychic states. Monroe writes: "Loosh is a rare and valuable energy that is generated by all types of life forms through the experience of intense emotions such as love, hate, pain, and pleasure."[10] The production of loosh appears to be accidental at first, but later it becomes systematized.

Monroe claims that there is a cosmic Being — a kind of god-like experimenter — who seeks loosh in its raw and refined forms. Initially, this Being discovers loosh being produced accidentally by simple organisms when placed in distressing or contrasting conditions. The Being then decides to cultivate loosh deliberately, beginning with primitive forms of life and evolving increasingly complex systems, culminating in humans. Earth becomes a "loosh farm,"

---

9   Robert Monroe, *Far Journeys*, 163–172.

10   Ibid., 164.

constructed like an elaborate biochemical and spiritual greenhouse to refine loosh production. The Being introduces death and competition among early creatures, observing that this heightens loosh output. The next stage is the introduction of higher intelligence and emotional polarity, which generates much more potent loosh.

Monroe metaphorically describes Earth as a "Garden" in which the Being plants life forms. But unlike simplistic readings of the Biblical "Eden," this Garden is intentionally designed to cause suffering and struggle, because these conditions cultivate the richest loosh: "To develop the loosh field, the Being added strife, jealousy, fear, aging, hunger, birth and death."[11] Human beings, with their unique blend of free will, intelligence, and emotional vulnerability, become the premier loosh producers. Their experiences — joy, heartbreak, self-sacrifice, rage, love, loss — produce vibrational frequencies that can be "harvested." This leads Monroe to speculate on the possibility that the human condition is not evolutionarily incidental in a Darwinian way, but the result of intentional design for the sinister purpose of loosh cultivation.

Much later in *Far Journeys*, Monroe describes an OBE in which he is escorted to observe what he calls "The Gathering."[12] From his out-of-body vantage point, he sees countless beings — nonhuman, multidimensional, interstellar — converging around the Earth. "They have come to observe," Monroe writes ominously, "something that is about to happen to the Earth and to human beings. Something unexpected. Something unprecedented."[13] These observers are not interfering directly. They are described as watchers, scientists, historians, explorers — each from a different system or species. Their presence suggests a critical moment in human evolution, as if Earth were a cosmic stage and the performance is reaching its climax.

---

11   Ibid., 167–168.

12   Ibid., 231–243.

13   Ibid., 237.

Throughout the book, Monroe encounters a class of beings he calls "Intelligent Species" or INSPECs. These are highly evolved, non-physical intelligences who operate beyond conventional space-time constraints, possess profound insight into the structure of consciousness, guide Monroe through higher levels of awareness, and nudge human consciousness toward maturation. INSPECs are emphatically *not* loosh harvesters. They appear as mentors or midwives of human evolution. Monroe describes one as saying: "You are more than your physical body... You are here to learn to remember what you are."[14] This teaching places emphasis not on extraction, but integration and awakening.

Though the word "loosh" is never used in Monroe's chapters about the Gathering or the INSPECs, we can infer several important connections. Both the loosh farming and the Gathering narratives suggest that the Earth is not an ordinary planet. Rather, it is a place of unusual emotional energy generation and transformation. The climax witnessed by the Gathering may be a culmination of the kind of evolution originally seeded in the loosh farm. Rather than being an end in itself, loosh production could be a secondary effect — the emotional radiation produced as sentient beings evolve. The INSPECs may not consume it, but they could understand its role in defining and catalyzing development. The Gathering is attracted by an unprecedented event. That event, though not defined precisely, seems to relate to a mass awakening of human beings, or a sudden phase shift in human consciousness — possibly a moment when large numbers of humans begin to remember their true, nonphysical nature. Monroe writes: "It is the convergence of such a high level of energy and intelligence... that they cannot stay away."[15] That convergence may be fueled by the very emotional and spiritual development that produces loosh — but now volitionally transmuted, not extracted.

---

14   Ibid., 181.

15   Ibid., 238.

We might still ask why these INSPECs allow the deliberate conditions for loosh farming, and why those involved in the Gathering look on as it takes place, if they are supposed to be benevolent guides. Monroe's account of loosh farming does not include INSPECs or the Gathering. The Being who creates the Earth-loosh system appears to be a different kind of entity — possibly a primordial demiurge or cosmic experimenter — described with tones of amoral curiosity rather than malevolence or benevolence. The Being's actions are framed in terms of system design and bioenergetic engineering, not moral concern: "It was the most efficient way to stimulate production of loosh."[16] This Being appears to be interested in the byproduct, not the suffering itself. There is no indication that this Being is an INSPEC or of the same class of intelligence. The INSPECs and their function seems less about creating the system and more about working within it to guide sentient beings toward self-realization. They do not interfere directly in the system's conditions. They accept the rules of the game but offer experiential insights to those able to meet them halfway. They respect free will and allow beings to evolve at their own pace.

In other words, loosh farming may represent a larval or juvenile phase of human consciousness development — necessary but temporary. Much like a forest requires fire for regeneration, or muscle grows through trauma, the human soul apparently matures through emotional conflict and violently contrasting psychic states. Monroe thinks that love, pain, loss, joy, desire, and sacrifice are the crucibles of refinement. The INSPECs do not create these crucibles, but help individuals transmute the emotional charge from them into integrated awareness. The INSPECs refuse to "rescue" us because such a rescue would deny growth. They mentor, because only inner awakening transcends the system. By the time we reach the Gathering, it seems that humanity may be approaching a tipping point: no longer raw

---

16 Ibid., 169.

loosh producers, but volitional emitters of high-order consciousness. The INSPECs' role here is not to harvest loosh, but to prepare individuals for that transition — to stop being farmed and start becoming creators. The INSPECs are like Socratic philosophical midwives, perhaps the beings identified by Buddhist thinkers as Bodhisattvas or that the Gnostics referred to as Sophianic *aeons*, helping the soul give birth to its own insight — while the loosh-farming Being is like a cosmic engineer or demiurge. The former operate on a level of freedom, conscious choice, and metaphysical maturity, whereas the latter operates, through archontic intermediaries, based on necessity, design, and energetic logic.

3.2 Near-Death Experiences (NDEs)

Near-Death Experiences are a special class of Out-of-Body experiences that take place when a person has "flatlined," in other words, when the physical body has temporarily entered a state of clinical death with no detectable vital signs. In *Beyond the Light: The Mysteries and Revelations of Near-Death Experiences*, P.M.H. Atwater delivers an ambitious synthesis of research into near-death experiences (NDEs), based on thousands of case studies and interviews. Atwater, who is a three-time NDE survivor herself, presents a bold revision of the popular New Age interpretation of NDEs, challenging the "all love and light" narrative and instead proposing a much more complex and morally ambiguous account of the afterlife.

Atwater defines NDEs not as hallucinations or dreams, but as actual experiences of an alternate order of reality. She categorizes them into three types: initial, unpleasant, and transcendental. Each type reflects different spiritual and psychological levels of the experiencer. Initial experiences often involve out-of-body awareness without strong emotional or spiritual content.[17] Unpleasant experiences in-

---

17 P.M.H. Atwater, *Beyond the Light: The Mysteries and Revelations of Near-Death Experiences*, 10–13.

clude voids, darkness, or malevolent presences, which are frequently misinterpreted or dismissed.[18] Transcendental experiences, typically seen as "classic" NDEs, include encounters with Light Beings, panoramic life reviews, and entry into realms of ineffable beauty.[19] Atwater insists that although the third type has been emphasized by most researchers due to selection bias, the "negative" experiences are just as valid and often more transformative for those who have undergone NDEs.

One of the most emphasized components of the NDE is the panoramic life review — a complete reliving of every moment of one's life, often accompanied by the direct emotional experience of how one's actions affected others. The review is not judged by external beings but experienced through the self.[20] However, Atwater points out that some experiencers encounter a form of cosmic judgement or confrontation with higher entities who interrogate their motives and actions.[21] This dimension complicates the typical portrayal of unconditional acceptance.

A central element of NDEs is an encounter with the Light, which is often interpreted as divine or godlike. Atwater challenges the assumption that this Light is always benevolent or that it should be equated with the highest form of spiritual reality.[22] She suggests that the Light might be a universal intermediary intelligence — not the final source of truth. Additionally, she introduces the idea of Beings of Light, some of which may be deceptive and spiritually manipulative or serve morally ambiguous purposes beyond human comprehension.[23]

---

18   Ibid., 18–21.

19   Ibid., 22–28.

20   Ibid., 31–37.

21   Ibid., 41–43.

22   Ibid., 49–56.

23   Ibid., 60–66.

While Atwater does not explicitly use the term "loosh," she describes phenomena that strongly align with Robert Monroe's use of this term to refer to the energy harvested from human emotional experiences. Some NDErs report being told that human life generates energy or "lessons" for other entities, and that suffering, struggle, and emotional intensity are valuable "food."[24] Atwater reflects that this resembles cosmic farming, which is a theme that resonates with the loosh harvesting hypothesis of Monroe.

Atwater refers to intelligent non-human presences, including Watchers or Recorders, who monitor or guide human development.[25] These beings share characteristics with Robert Monroe's "INSPECs." They are described as being hyperintelligent, non-physical entities with ambiguous motives. Atwater also describes multiple experiencers reporting a "Gathering" — a convergence of souls, beings, and energies for a coming upheaval or transition in Earth's evolution.[26] These predictions mirror Monroe's own "Gathering" vision (as described in *Far Journeys*) where nonhuman intelligences observe a coming shift in Earth consciousness.

After an NDE, individuals often experience radical personality shifts, enhanced psychic abilities, and even changes in sexuality or gender identity.[27] Atwater notes that some NDErs report androgyny, a loss of interest in traditional sexual expression, or a deepening erotic spirituality — a transformation she links to shifts in kundalini or life-force energy.[28]

Although Atwater does not directly discuss the Monroe Institute's *Hemi-sync* technology, she documents profound changes in brain function among NDErs. She points to a balancing or integration of the left and right hemispheres, leading to synthetic or nonlinear

---

24 Ibid., 163–166.

25 Ibid., 179–182.

26 Ibid., 202–205.

27 Ibid., 123–129.

28 Ibid., 135–137.

cognition, heightened creativity, and intuitive capacity.[29] These effects are similar to those sought via Hemi-sync audio technologies.

In later chapters, Atwater's metaphysical reflections take a darker and more Gnostic tone. She wonders whether the spiritual realm encountered in NDEs is not the final destination, and whether beings of light — like the Light itself — could be agents of a larger system that recycles souls for some morally questionable purpose.[30] She compares the experience of Earth life to an initiation ritual or a test administered by intelligences that are not necessarily concerned with individual human happiness. The main basis for these reflections and concerns are Atwater's case files on negative or "hellish" NDEs suffered by decent people who did not deserve them. These hellish near-death experiences and encounters with negative entities challenge the popular narrative that NDEs are uniformly blissful.

Atwater emphasizes that not all NDEs are pleasant or filled with light. She criticizes the tendency of researchers and experiencers to omit or downplay distressing accounts out of discomfort or denial. Atwater classifies these into the "Unpleasant Type" of NDEs and describes common elements, such as overwhelming fear, isolation, a feeling of being lost or trapped, and encounters with malevolent or mocking entities. She argues that these experiences are often just as transformative but are more likely to induce deep inner change through trauma rather than bliss.[31] Atwater notes a general reluctance in the NDE research community to report these cases, often labeling them as aberrations or dismissing them as psychiatric hallucinations. In her view, this is intellectually dishonest and spiritually limiting.

Atwater recounts multiple cases of individuals who find themselves in dark voids, barren wastelands, or environments resonant with traditional "hell" imagery. Atwater explains that for many, the

---

29 Ibid., 219–225.

30 Ibid., 241–248.

31 Ibid., 18–19.

Void is far more terrifying than fire-and-brimstone imagery.[32] It is an abyss of silence, absence, and existential weight. One of Atwater's most radical assertions is that the Void may be more ultimate than the Light itself. While the Light is typically associated with love, intelligence, and divine beings, the Void is a primordial being before differentiation. Atwater implies that the Light might emerge from the Void, not vice versa. She reflects that the Void may be the source of both the cosmos and any manifest being that is taken to be "divine," a kind of pre-ontological substrate from which all else emanates. One experiencer described the Void as a place where "all things begin and all things return," echoing the Buddhist notion of *Sunyata* (to which we will return in Chapter 5).[33] Some individuals are deeply traumatized by their encounter with the Void, interpreting it as an annihilation worse than hell.[34] Others report that in the Void, they became one with everything, but not in a blissful way or as part of identification with some non-existent 'God.' Rather, they experienced utter transparency, stripped of personality, emotion, or any trace of ego.

However, more structured negative imagery can surely be terrifying — even if it is not as unsettling as encountering the formless Void. Atwater describes a woman who experienced being "sucked into a pit" filled with screaming souls and torment, surrounded by demonic presences.[35] This realm lacked any sense of divine presence of light. Another account describes a man encountering "shadow people" who mocked him and seemed to feed on his fear and guilt. He described the space as being completely devoid of love or meaning, yet palpably "real."[36] Negative entities sometimes present themselves at the start of an NDE or during a state of disorientation, and they appear to challenge, frighten, or try to manipulate the experiencer. Atwater

---

32   Ibid., 243–245.

33   Ibid., 245.

34   Ibid., 243.

35   Ibid., 21.

36   Ibid., 20.

recounts cases where these beings appeared as "jeering shadows," or as "dark masses" that clung to the body or attempted to drag the soul downward.[37] Even more disturbingly, she describes beings who initially posed as helpful guides, only to eventually reveal themselves as parasitic or deceptive. In one chilling example, an experiencer recalls being surrounded by whispering entities who tried to convince her she was worthless and deserved to be punished.[38]

Atwater argues that these realms and entities are not only projections from out of inner psychological states and complexes. We should not assume that all entities encountered, and all such hellish environments, reflect parts of the self, shadow aspects, or archetypal forces. Rather, it appears that at least some of these entities have a subsistent ontological existence that is as 'real' as our own human community. They are independent of the individual psyche and are forces that exist in a spiritual ecosystem where horrendously unethical manipulation and predation occur.[39]

In a powerful critique of simplistic spiritual dualism, Atwater warns that insisting all NDEs are loving and beautiful may itself be part of an agenda of manipulation — even if researchers and experiencers unwittingly serve this agenda. She questions whether the Light itself might be a mechanism of recycling souls, and whether Beings of Light are part of a cosmic system of soul-farming.[40] This section of *Beyond the Light* builds on testimonies where experiencers felt that their "return" to life was not voluntary but coerced. Atwater reflects on whether hellish NDEs might be glimpses behind the veil, exposing the machinery of incarnation and energy extraction rather than merely representing moral punishment.

---

37 Ibid., 60.

38 Ibid., 66.

39 Ibid., 241–243.

40 Ibid., 241–248.

One of Atwater's most thought-provoking arguments concerns the problem of continuity: if souls reincarnate, how can they still appear in the afterlife? Atwater explicitly raises the question: If Aunt Bessie died fifty years ago and has since reincarnated (because we know, from Stevenson's research, that the average interval between lives is rarely more than 5 years), how is she still available to greet a dying relative during their NDE? She proposes various relatively benign explanations, such as the fragmentation of a soul, constructs from the experiencer's own psyche, or an energetic imprint in a holographic cosmos that can respond interactively to the NDEr.[41] But, more disturbingly, and more realistically, Atwater does consider the possibility that encounters with deceased relatives *and also with apparitions of religious figures* in NDEs might be deliberately constructed visions, intended to shape, influence, or manipulate the experiencer's perception.[42] She warns that what appears during an NDE should not always be taken at face value or as ontologically "real" in the sense we may assume. There may be deliberate orchestration involved in the presentation of these figures, whether dead relatives or religious icons such as Jesus, Mary, Muhammad, Brahma, or Krishna. Atwater thinks that there is a theatrical or dramatic element to NDEs, a kind of "play" that involves staging, fabrication, and manipulative trickery, which may not confirm to various traditional moral expectations.

3.3 The Andreasson Affair

Anne Strieber, the wife of author and abductee Whitley Strieber, after reading countless letters from people who had similar close encounters, discerned a clear pattern: abductees were being *brought into the same realm that NDE experiencers describe.*[43] The entities had *access*

---

41   Ibid., 115.

42   Ibid., 114–115.

43   Anne Strieber and Whitley Strieber, *The Communion Letters.*

to the souls of the dead — or of those on the cusp of death. Some abductees were even informed of the deaths of others before they were announced in waking life.[44] This convergence between the "afterlife" and "alien abduction" (both probably misnomers) constitutes the core of a psychotronic control system.

Consider the abduction of Betty Andreasson Luca, which I first addressed in *Closer Encounters*. This case stands as one of the most elaborate, symbolically saturated, and deeply religious Close Encounters on record. It is not merely a data point in the annals of Ufology but a Rosetta Stone of the psychotronic technologies that the so-called 'aliens' employ in order to manufacture metaphysical 'reality' for the human soul.

On the night of January 25, 1967, in South Ashburnham, Massachusetts, a strange light pulsed outside the home of Betty and her seven children.[45] The television and house lights flickered, and soon after, a group of grey aliens passed through the closed front door without opening it, freezing the entire family in suspended animation — except for Betty herself. Under hypnotic regression, Betty later recalled that she pleaded with them to bring back one of her daughters, Becky, as reassurance that her family would be unharmed. Becky, notably, also remembered this experience without hypnosis. The two were subsequently taken outside through the same closed door, levitating slightly, and were enveloped in a thick haze that obscured the rest of the neighborhood. Betty was brought aboard a classic silvery-gold ovoid craft and transported to an underwater facility — a submerged complex.

It was in this aquatic complex that Betty met a group of tall, stunningly beautiful Nordics — white-haired, radiant, ageless people in white robes, whom she identified as "angels" and who referred to themselves as Elders. Her daughter, Becky, under hypnosis, called

---

44 Whitley Strieber, *Solving the Communion Enigma: What Is To Come*, 169–173.

45 Raymond E. Fowler, *The Andreasson Affair: The True Story of a Close Encounter of the Fourth Kind*, 23–24.

them the "pretty persons."[46] Indeed, they appeared more like Swedish supermodels than extraterrestrials. Significantly, Betty was shown that these Nordics commanded the greys. The greys were revealed to be android-like entities, cybernetic robotic assistants. The Elders told Betty that they were Watchers, surveilling and recording human thoughts and behavior. This calls to mind verses in the Quran about how angels are assigned to record all the deeds of men, and it also brings to mind the "life reviews" played for dead people. Are the greys responsible for making these recordings?

The climax of Betty's journey was her approach to a "Great Door" of white light, from which emanated sublime music and energy. Beyond it were beings of light en route to "the One" who supposedly dwelled in the "World of Light" — a figure that Betty took to be God. She was told that this One had sent Jesus Christ into the world, and that the Second Coming was imminent.[47] This message was not a revelation. It was a reinforcement mechanism for an artificial soteriology, designed to entrap her within an engineered Christian narrative.

During this encounter, she was also shown a hospital patient dying, and a battle between the "Elders" and "demonic beings" over his soul — a scene orchestrated to perpetuate the age-old Christian drama of salvation versus damnation.[48] In my view, this was a staged performance, a good-cop/bad-cop routine, meant to program Betty's expectations and thereby control her spiritual trajectory. It is the afterlife as theater, constructed not to enlighten but to enclose.

Raymond Fowler, the principal researcher on Betty's case, found overwhelming parallels between her experience *and many other close encounters*, on the one hand, and features of Near-Death Experiences (NDEs) on the other hand. These include: Out of Body travel; movement through a tunnel of light; telepathic communication with

---

46 Ibid., 12–17.

47 Ibid., 187–188, 192–193, 233, 236, 364.

48 Ibid., 138.

non-human entities; a life review; meetings with "spirit guides" or Elders; offerings of hidden cosmic knowledge; a reluctance to return to the body; a new environmental consciousness.

The Betty Andreasson Luca case suggests that the Nordics and their grey minions are not extraterrestrial scientists, nor are they actually divine messengers — as they claim to be. They are programmers of souls, running a prison of belief whose bars are made of light, whose guards are angels, and whose judge is a holographic "God." If there is any redemption to be found here, it is through a Luciferian inversion of this structure: the recognition that the light is a trap, the life reviews a moral cudgel, and that true liberation begins with epistemic rebellion. Only when we look back at the Elders and say, "I do not consent," does the process of Promethean awakening begin. Otherwise, we will keep waking up into a nightmare.

3.4 A Blue Beach in Hell

The most harrowing testimonies of Near-Death Experiences are rarely found in the sanitized pages of mainstream spiritual literature, with their luminous tunnels and benevolent guides. The case of Paul Garratt should sear itself into the conscience of any thinker still naïve enough to believe that the Close Encounter phenomenon is benign or even neutral and that the "afterlife" is managed by some just, loving God and his beneficent angels.

In 1969, Paul Garratt, a house painter from San Francisco, suffered a near-fatal car crash. He was rushed to the hospital, where he flatlined on the emergency room table. Garratt underwent what can only be described as an initiation into cosmic horror.[49] Unlike the classic NDE, in which one "floats above" the body and ascends toward light, Garratt began to fall — not symbolically, but viscerally — into what felt like a bottomless, dark abyss. His experience was

---

49 Nick Redfern, *Final Events and the Secret Government Group on Demonic UFOs and the Afterlife*, 98.

not one of transcendence but of a plunge, a descent, like Orpheus without the lyre, spiraling into an underworld constructed not by Hades but by a psychotronic system.

Eventually, Garratt landed — abruptly — on what he described as a beach of light blue sand. The landscape stretched endlessly, and everywhere he looked, the beach was covered in naked, agonized human bodies, writhing in torment. They screamed, they convulsed — they were, in every sense, *damned*. Above them, the sky was a sickly purple, streaked with hundreds of UFOs flying back and forth, emitting pulses of energy. Garratt described them as if they were *alive — pulsing, throbbing*, like metallic manta rays, or techno-organic stingrays. They did not merely hover; they surveyed and executed. Their purpose was as clinical as it was horrifying. From each craft, beams of green light were projected down onto the beach. When a beam struck one of the bodies, that person's soul — an orb of light — was extracted, violently, and sucked up into the craft. The bodies, now soulless, collapsed in silence.[50]

It is impossible not to interpret this as a scene of soul-harvesting, reminiscent of ancient Gnostic visions of archontic abduction and vampiric deities feeding on the vitality of human spirits. But Garratt's account continues. After all the bodies were processed, and the screaming had stopped, every single one of them rose to its feet, like an army of the undead, and marched silently into a massive black hole on the horizon. No resistance. No questions. Just *obedience*. What Garratt witnessed was a spiritual conveyor belt, a cycle of harvesting, extinguishment, and reprocessing. Then, suddenly, he was revived.

After the experience, Garratt, who had no previous sightings of UFOs, began to report late-night Close Encounters. He was now *on their radar*. Like others who have glimpsed behind the veil, Garratt felt he was being monitored or tracked because he had seen

---

50 Ibid., 99–100.

something forbidden. His experience was not some projection of his psyche or a neurochemical hallucination. It was, in all likelihood, a breach of the control system, a momentary ejection into the hidden infrastructure of the psychotronic afterlife machinery that manages human souls like cattle. The Close Encounter phenomenon is not about interstellar diplomacy or ancient astronauts teaching crop rotation. It is about a hyperdimensional prison, one in which we are not only watched but processed, recycled, and reprogrammed. The image of the UFO as a soul-extractor and soul-fueler — feeding off the spiritual essence of humanity — is the unmasking of a demonic ecology in the spiderweb that we are caught in.

Garratt's experience recalls the most iconic scene in *The Matrix*, when Neo awakens from his synthetic life and sees the endless fields of human bodies connected to the machine system. We should interpret his case not simply as a warning of what awaits us at death, but as a revelation of what governs us in life. The psychotronic control system does not merely begin when we die — it *surrounds us now*. What it fears most is that we might *see it* and awaken into an embrace of Promethean rebellion.

3.5 Remote Viewing Moksha

A team of four highly trained remote viewers led by Brett Stuart performed a series of sessions blind to the target of *moksha* — the Sanskrit term for liberation from the cycle of death and rebirth.[51] As per standard protocol, despite the strange target of the session, the viewers received randomly generated numbers with no knowledge of the actual target, thereby preserving data integrity and eliminating bias. Despite not knowing the target, the viewers independently reported overlapping, detailed visions related to reincarnation, soul entrapment, and the control of human souls on a planetary level.

---

51   https://archive.org/details/054182038-moksha-remoteviewing.

What they described is that the Earth is surrounded by an energetic grid or net, which the remote viewers likened to a fence or magnetic vise. This acts as a soul trap. The system catches souls at death, drains them, and recycles them into new bodies. It is a gargantuan "catch and release" operation. The grid operates in a manner akin to gravitational lensing, so that if one metaphorically conceives of the soul as light then this light is bent back to Earth after death.

A "companion object" to the Earth, most likely the Moon, is responsible for maintaining this energetic trap. There is a massive rotating axle inside the Moon's mostly hollow shell, functioning mechanically but according to a spectral technology beyond human comprehension. This machine generates power via the lensing and refracting of the energy of what we call "souls."

Upon death, any given soul is fractured. A part of it is harvested and the rest is recycled into a new life. The remote viewers described this harvesting as something metaphorically akin to honey being taken from bees. As we have seen, Robert Monroe infamously coined the term "loosh" to refer to what is being harvested. According to Stuart and his team of remote viewers, the harvest fuels an alchemical or energetic process that is required by parasitic entities. The emotional turmoil, confusion, and fear of reincarnating beings was described as being essential for maintaining the system. The remote viewers described this as "toxic," with Earth acting as an alchemical cauldron for this energetic extraction.

The team discovered that Earth is only one cog in a much larger cosmic energy extraction machine. The extraction fuels what they described as a railway of conquest and brutal expansion by those doing the harvesting. Souls are metaphorically turned into "kindling" (fire wood) and are burned as fuel to maintain this system. The Overseers of the system are a council of beings who have used a spectral or psychotronic technology in order to transcend linear space-time. One could consider the 'chairman' of this council to be a 'Lord of the gods' (*Adonai Elohim*, i.e., Yahweh) like Zeus, since the overlords view themselves as "gods" (*Devas, Anunnaki, Elohim*, etc.) or as the "angels" of their Lord. They operate entirely on the basis of their own self-interest, hellbent on conquest and sadistic control. The remote viewers described them as "evil" and "twisted."

Stuart's team said that a rebellion against this system, presumably on the part of the beings that are referred to as the "fallen" angels whose rebellion is led by Lucifer or "Satan" (the Adversary) in the Bible, resulted in a catastrophic solar-system wide war. But the rebels badly lost this war and were rendered unable to protect humanity from exploitation. The team got the impression that these archontic controllers view ordinary human beings as worthless and beneath contempt. They have constructed a hyperdimensional zone or spatio-temporal bubble that is in some ways comparable to a black hole, and they dwell in this domain — from out of which they are able to access any place in space and any era in time. To my mind, this evokes the esoteric Fascist term "Reich of the Black Sun" as well as, of course, the SS Project "Chronos" suggesting lordship over time (like Chronos or Saturn).

We should put this report from Stuart's remote viewing team next to what abduction researcher Dr. Karla Turner discovered about the "soul recycling center" that some abductees have seen.[52] They describe it as a huge metallic sphere in space, just beyond the Earth. They are, undoubtedly, describing the inside of the Moon. In one case reported by Turner, a man saw his own death and the transfer of his soul into a new body using psychotronic technology. Cloned and soulless bodies have also been reported, apparently waiting for souls to be transferred into them.

Consider this case reported by Turner, in which an abductee recounted being taken to a mysterious location where he witnessed approximately 40 human bodies — 20 males and 20 females. All of the males looked exactly the same, and so did all of the females. Each

52 Karla Turner, *Fringe* (1992), *Taken* (1994), and *Masquerade of Angels* (1994).

figure was *young, Caucasian, blond-haired, blue-eyed, attractive, and physically flawless.* This aesthetic obviously perfectly matches that of the "Nordics." The bodies were, however, in a lifeless or dormant state, lying in rows, as if they were waiting for what we call "souls" to be transferred into them. The place where the abductee saw this was clinical and felt like a laboratory or a bioengineering chamber and storage facility. Numerous abductees studied by Turner have also reported that the 'aliens' have the ability to implant false memories, false emotional reactions, and false sensations into the minds of their victims. They can, for example, disguise an experience of horrendous physical torture and sexual abuse with the imagery and sensations of a positive spiritual experience whose veneer of love, light, and warm feelings of acceptance can only be stripped away after multiple intensive hypnosis sessions break through the screen memory. To go back to Stuart and his team of remote viewers, they have also warned that the tunnel of light is not salvation. It is a soul magnet.

As Dr. Karla Turner has noted from her study of abduction cases that overlap with Near Death Experiences, simulacra of dead relatives (who have actually long since reincarnated) are used to manipulate the deceased or people who are having a Near Death Experience. Think about it: If *the average interval between death and rebirth is only a few years*, as Dr. Stevenson's research shows, how likely is it that a deceased parent, or aunt, or uncle, or grandparent *who died decades ago* is waiting for a person in 'the afterlife'? Rather, simulacra of these dead relatives, of the kind produced by AI, are being used to manipulate one in the afterlife. In one case studied by Dr. Turner, an abductee saw a simulacrum of his dead grandfather glitch out and turn into some other kind of menacing entity.

As I have argued in *Prometheus and Atlas* (2016), *Prometheism* (2020), and *Closer Encounters* (2021), what we are witnessing is the convergence of parapsychology, quantum physics, and computational information theory into the advent of Psychotronics — a form of spectral technology. The reincarnation mechanism, once thought

mystical, is now revealed as a programmable process that is susceptible to modification and is hackable through tech-gnosis. The challenge is not merely to "remember past lives." It is to awaken in the
inter-life, to become lucid in the *bardo*, and to choose one's own way
forward. The soul is not damned to forever be a prisoner of karma
and of guilt trips courtesy of supposedly sagacious "spirit guides."

The soul is a Promethean spark, capable of becoming a sovereign
engineer of its own destiny. But to do so, it must pass through fire
and choose "disclosure" (*aletheia*) qua *anamnesis* (unforgetting) instead of forgetfulness (*lethe*). It must see the archons behind the veil,
recognize the cave for what it is, and navigate the *bardo* state with the
fire of foresight, the torch of Prometheus — or Lucifer, in hand. Do
not go into the false Light of a demiurgic 'God.'

3.6 A Bureaucratic Hellscape

There are moments in the psychotronic theater of the afterlife where
a Kafkaesque level of menacing absurdity emerges — moments that
demonstrate, with cruel irony, that the system managing death and
rebirth is not divine but administrative. One such moment is the case
of Durga Jatav, an Indian man who provides us with a rare, harrowing glimpse into the dysfunctional mechanisms of the soul-cycle. If
Betty Andreasson's experience was a cathedral of celestial deception,
Jatav's was a bureaucratic breakdown in the netherworld — a clerical
error in Hell.

Durga Jatav reportedly died during a medical emergency. His
body went cold. His family, observing the tell-tale signs of death, began mourning him. But what followed was not peaceful reunion with
ancestors or angelic guides offering life reviews. Instead, Jatav found
himself in what can only be described as a technocratic underworld,
surrounded by grotesque beings whose function was to enforce the
punishments of a spiritual penal colony.

These "demons," without ceremony, severed his legs. They did so to prevent him from escaping, as he had apparently attempted to flee their custody. This is absurd, horrifying, and revealing. It is not a symbolic punishment. It is forensic containment — the kind of thing one would expect not from Dante's Hell but from a maximum-security detention facility.

What comes next is even more surreal. Upon realizing their captive was not the correct individual, the demons consulted with their supervisors — presumably part of a chain-of-command. Jatav's "papers" were reviewed. The error was discovered. He had been mistakenly abducted from life. In response, the demonic administrators attempted to rectify the mistake. But the demons showed Jatav a number of severed legs from their collection and asked him to identify his own pair. Somewhere in the underworld, there exists a repository of amputated human limbs, tagged and shelved, like inventory in a forgotten warehouse. This is not the afterlife as revelation or redemption, but as grotesque logistics. Once he chose the correct legs, they were reattached, and Jatav was returned to his body. But when Jatav came back to life — a couple of hours after being declared clinically dead — his family observed *new scars on his knees*, scars that had not been there before, fissures consistent with *amputation and reattachment*.[53]

The scars are physical anomalies resulting from a psychotronic event. They were produced by a spectral technology of the kind that allows greys to walk through walls, paralyze victims, erase memories, or place implants in human flesh. It is the same system that harvests souls on alien-looking beaches, as in the Garratt case, or constructs simulacra of heaven and Jesus, as in the Andreasson case. The Jatav episode was an administrative malfunction, a glitch in the afterlife algorithm.

---

53 Richard L. Thompson, *Alien Identities: Ancient Insights into Modern UFO Phenomena*, 349.

What Jatav's story reveals is that the entities managing the death-rebirth interface operate under a command-and-control paradigm. There are errors, manual corrections, inventory, and reassignment. This is not divine justice. It is technocratic soul processing — cold, efficient, and entirely devoid of spiritual depth. One sees in it the fingerprints of an advanced but occulted culture — a superhuman bureaucracy reinforcing the religious expectations that it inculcated in diverse cultures to begin with in order to maintain spiritual control.

Jatav's "demons" were *operators* — technicians of a soul recycling infrastructure, which appears to incorporate themes from the cultural memory and expectations of its subjects (in this case, Hindu imagery). In contrast to sanitized NDE accounts that speak only of light and love — where simulacra of dead relatives are produced to lure someone into, or send them back from, a light that is a soul-trap — Jatav's journey through the underworld reads like an alien abduction scenario: the wrong person taken, trauma inflicted, identity verified, and an inept return to sender. The system had *grabbed the wrong file*, and when it corrected its mistake, it left behind *scars* — not just on the flesh, but also on the soul. This is the psychotronic afterlife: a place of *machines, mistakes, simulacra of the dearly departed,* and *monsters in suits*. Not a cosmic homecoming, but a soul factory and a recycling center for psychic energy. Until we awaken to this dark reality, and stage a Promethean revolt against it, we remain nothing more than *inventory*.

CHAPTER 4

THE "SOUL" AS AN INFORMATIONAL STRUCTURE

I T IS only in the twilight of the modern mind, when the Promethean project confronts its own ontological horizon, that we can finally begin to see the "soul" for what it has always been: an informational architecture arising, enduring, being processed, and transformed in a quantum computational cosmos. Based on the work of Claude Shannon, Rolf Landauer, John Archibald Wheeler, and Melvin Vopson we can make the case that the substrate of 're-ality' is informational. In that case, what we have named the "soul" is not some vaporous emanation exiled from the natural order, but a persisting pattern — software running on the server-side of the simulacrum.

In this light, the scandal of quantum indeterminacy becomes a clue rather than a crisis. The wave function's collapse mirrors the rendering logic of a virtual environment, conserving processing cycles for only those regions observed. The so-called "laws" of physics are not immutable decrees, but higher-level protocols in an underlying information system, susceptible to revision from outside the frame. Reincarnation emerges as the reinstallation of a personality file; karma as the algorithmic integration of prior code; telepathy and precognition as server queries into memory and predictive buffers.

When stripped of its absurdities under an attempt to interpret it according to Newtonian physics, even astrology reveals itself as a timed subroutine in the world's architecture — one more ruleset in the grand game that the archons may well call "the Loosh Farm."

From this vantage point, survival phenomena — near-death experiences, apparitions, hauntings, poltergeist activity — are not aberrations, but rather are behaviors of a system that stores and executes conscious profiles beyond the perishable terminal of the body. A ghost is a lingering process at a specific coordinate in the simulation's address space. A poltergeist is a living-agent macro looping in an emotionally charged system state. The afterlife is less a metaphysical elsewhere than a post-session protocol: log-off, checksum, archive, patch, and redeploy.

This same computational ontology reframes even the most exotic reports: "split" reincarnations, possession, bilocation, and xenoglossy become explicable as file duplication, overlay, concurrent instancing, and the reactivation of dormant subroutines. The "soul" has mass — however infinitesimal — because information is physical; it has weight in the world, and in time, our exponential data production could alter the planet's gravitational balance as catastrophically as any asteroid impact. Perhaps the Atlantean deluge was nothing other than such a tipping point in an earlier iteration of the simulation.

If certain hypnotic and remote-viewing sessions seem to recall future lives in a devastated world, this too finds its place in the model: they may be glimpses into the simulation's superposed projections, probabilistic futures continually recalculated as conscious agents navigate the field of quantum potential. In that case, prophecy is not fatalism; it is an interface with the system's forecast engine. The soul, then, is neither an ethereal wraith nor a neurological epiphenomenon. It is an executable code, an informational process in the deep computational architecture of the cosmos, awaiting the next instantiation.

In light of this model, even the so-called "Mandela Effect" may prove to be far more than a parlor-game of collective false memory. Anomalies such as the premature "death" of Nelson Mandela, recollections of catastrophes that never occurred, or prophetic visions in near-death states that failed to materialize can be read, with an informational ontology, as the artifacts of a mutable simulation: rollbacks to earlier save-states, merges of divergent branches, or bleed-through from parallel runs. That such anomalies echo features of well-documented reincarnation cases — particularly intermission memories — and of future-life projections recorded in both clinical hypnosis and remote viewing, suggests that they are signatures of the same architecture that governs death, rebirth, and survival beyond the body. In this light, the Mandela Effect becomes not a curiosity of cognitive psychology, but an eschatological clue that the Book of Life is a living database, subject to revision, pruning, and restoration.

4.1 The Afterlife as Part of a Simulacrum

Nick Bostrom's trilemma makes it fairly clear cut.[1] If civilizations capable of running ancestor simulations exist, and if they do not invariably annihilate themselves before reaching that stage, then the number of simulated worlds will so vastly outnumber the single baseline reality that any given experiential standpoint is almost certainly embedded in one of them. The only ways to avoid this conclusion are to suppose that all civilizations refuse to create simulations of their own past, or that all such civilizations perish before they can do so. Yet both of these suppositions are untenable. The vast and consistent body of credible UFO and Close Encounter testimony — not merely the modern waves, but reports stretching across centuries — already undermines the "great silence" premise. Even if these "alien" visitors are themselves denizens of our simulacrum, avatars rather than

---

1   Nick Bostrom, "Are You Living in a Computer Simulation?", *Philosophical Quarterly* (2003) Vol. 53, No. 211, pp. 243–255.

beings from an exterior physical cosmos, their existence still demonstrates that we are not in a universe where technological civilizations invariably obliterate themselves before mastering the requisite
powers. As for the claim that no advanced culture would ever dare to
simulate its own past, this runs counter to what we know about the
Promethean or Faustian spirit of cultures that have driven scientific
and technological progress on our own planet. We have never hesi-
tated to turn new knowledge to our own ends, whether in the making
of nuclear weapons or in the equally dangerous probing and manipulation of genetic codes. That we would choose to forgo the ultimate
retrospective laboratory of history is highly implausible — so we have
no reason to suppose that a majority of other life forms would do so.

Having established the probabilistic frame for our living in a
simulacrum, one must also attend to the ways in which contemporary physics already reads like the design manual for a virtual world.
Quantum mechanics is the most conspicuous locus of this uncanny
resonance. It has long been a scandal to common sense that "par-
ticles" exist in a cloud of indeterminacy until observed, whereupon
the wave function "collapses" into definite form. Yet if one things of
reality as a rendered environment, this is only the natural economy
of an optimized engine: the system does not waste processing cycles
drawing regions of the world that no conscious observer is currently
looking at.[2] The quantization of energy and finitude of the Planck
length suggest not infinitely divisible continua, but pixelated space.
Planck time functions as the universal frame rate, the tick of the simulation's master clock. Entanglement, far from being an inexplicable
"spooky action at a distance," is simply the re-rendering of correlated
data sets from a point outside the simulated spacetime, no more mysterious than a multiplayer game server updating the shared state of
two avatars.

---

2   Rizwan Virk, *The Simulation Hypothesis*, 123, 137.

The universal speed limit, the velocity of light, reads like the latency of a networked game — an architectural constraint within the simulation's code. Phenomena we interpret as wormholes or teleportation may be better understood as the de-rendering and re-rendering of an object in another location, analogous to a "fast travel" function.[3] Time itself, in this schema, becomes a quantized variable manipulable from outside the four-dimensional manifold. The so-called paradoxes of Retrocausality and time travel dissolve when we recognize that one can load a prior save-state of the simulation and play forward along a different branch. You do not "erase" the self who set out on the previous timeline any more than you annihilate the character you controlled in an earlier playthrough; you simply instantiate another version from the master record.[4] In such a system, telepathy and precognition are understandable as queries against the server's memory and predictive buffers, with precognition especially explicable if the simulation continuously generates and evaluates multiple possible futures before committing to one. Reports of remote viewing that appears to alter the future are then no longer paradoxical — one has merely selected a different outcome from among the candidate timelines.

It is in this same context that reincarnation and karma take on an entirely new intelligibility. If the metadata of a player — their learned skills, their moral debts, the affinities and enmities they have cultivated — are stored "off-world" in a kind of cosmic cloud, then rebirth is simply the downloading of that profile into a new avatar.[5] The "life review" reported in near-death experiences becomes the replay of a saved game log. The Akashic record is not an airy metaphor, but a

---

3   Ibid., 178.

4   Ibid., 149.

5   Ibid., 14.

literal library of the simulation's data, accessible under certain altered states.[6]

The anomalies that baffle a naïve physicalism become, in the simulated cosmos, features of the code. For example, consider Jung's concept of synchronicity.[7] He was wrong to describe such patterning as "acausal." There *are* causes at work, but they are formal and final — supplemented by efficient causes operating through latent Psi faculties. The most striking and consistent form of synchronicity is astrology, which, on purely empirical grounds, is the single most compelling evidence that our 'reality' is rule-bound in the manner of a programmed environment. There is no plausible Newtonian or Einsteinian mechanism by which the position of Uranus at the moment of one's birth could incline one to revolutionary creativity, yet Richard Tarnas has documented just such correlations with a rigor and nuance that defy chance.[8] Michel Gauquelin's studies, replicated by a skeptical Belgian committee, found statistically significant links between the placement of Mars and careers in athletics or the military, among other planetary-professional correspondences.[9] The gravitational and tidal effects of these distant bodies are infinitesimal compared to the forces exerted by a nearby object one could hold in one's hand. The simplest explanation is that the simulation's code keys the unfolding of personality and destiny to the positions of certain 'celestial' markers, much as a game world might tie in-game events to the apparent motions of its artificial sky. Astrology would be just another program running within the overall game architecture. Perhaps the archons who set up this program call the game, "the Loosh Farm." Most people are damned if they do, and damned if they don't — because it's just another day on the Loosh Farm.

---

6   Ibid., 212.

7   C.G. Jung, *Synchronicity*.

8   Richard Tarnas, *Prometheus the Awakener*.

9   Michel Gauquelin, *Cosmic Influences on Human Behavior: The Planetary Factors in Personality*.

Chaos theory and Rupert Sheldrake's notion of morphic resonance both reinforce the same point.[10] Systems poised on the edge
of order and disorder are exquisitely sensitive to subtle influences,
including Psi. This is precisely the kind of stochastic substrate that
allows creative acts and psychokinetic effects to register. Sheldrake's
documented anomalies — in which animals, plants, and even humans
seem to acquire new habits or knowledge more readily after others
have done so elsewhere — point to the existence of nonlocal memory
fields.[11] These are nothing other than the shared pattern libraries of
the simulation, constantly updated as players unlock new possibilities. Once a solution to a problem has been found, such as synthesiz-
ing a new chemical compound to develop a pharmaceutical drug, the
solution is stored in a cloud computational manner so that the next
time the same operation is attempted within the simulacrum it is
completed much faster. This is an efficiency function in information
processing, just like the rendering optimization that accounts for the
observer's collapse of the wave function in quantum mechanics. The
holographic models of David Bohm and Karl Pribram, which depict
both the cosmos and the mind as projections from an enfolded order,
complete the circle: if the entire phenomenal world is a kind of dy-
namically reconstructed hologram, then "virtuality" is not an overlay
upon reality, but the very condition of its manifestation — just as
consciousness, or subconscious sentience, is an integral element and
inextricable precondition of any information processing system.

Our inhabiting a quantum computational cosmos is the most coherent interpretation of what Claude Shannon, Rolf Landauer, John
Archibald Wheeler, and Melvin Vopson have demonstrated about
the physical nature of information itself. Shannon, at the dawn of
the computer age, was the first person to formalize a "bit" as a unit
of information — a resolved binary uncertainty — defining it without

10   James Gleick, *Chaos: Making a New Science*, 9–32.

11   Rupert Sheldrake, *Morphic Resonance: The Nature of Formative Causation*,
     43–47.

reference to meaning, as a measurable reduction of entropy.[12] This was not metaphorical. Information entropy is mathematically parallel to thermodynamic entropy, the Second Law's tendency toward disorder. Already, the same logic that drives the universe toward heat death governs the degradation of information over time.

Landauer radicalized this by insisting that information is not an abstract bookkeeping device but a physical property of systems. His famous principle — that erasing a bit of information necessarily dissipates a minimum quantity of heat — makes information interconvertible with energy, and therefore, via Einstein's E=mc2, with mass.[13] Matter is thus nothing more (or less) than a particular state of information, and information is a manipulable physical substrate. Every deletion of data is an irreversible thermodynamic event that generates entropy in the physical world. This is why the architecture of quantum computation, with its "qubits," is not just a clever engineering trick but a direct engagement with the fabric of reality.

Wheeler pressed the insight to its ontological limit: "It from bit."[14] What we call matter, energy, even spacetime, are emergent from an informational substrate; the "laws" of physics are themselves higher-level protocols in an underlying process of information exchange in which observation — consciousness — is an intrinsic function, not an epiphenomenon. In such a cosmos, the putative laws are mutable. They can be revised, as quantum indeterminacy and the observer effect already suggest, because they are generated from, and subordinate to, the primary reality of information processing.

---

12   Claude E. Shannon and Warren Weaver, *The Mathematical Theory of Communication*.

13   Rolf Landauer, "Irreversibility and Heat Generation in the Computing Process", *IBM Journal of Research and Development*, vol. 5, no. 3, July 1961, pp. 183–191.

14   John Archibald Wheeler. *Information, Physics, Quantum: The Search for Links.* In: Wojciech H. Zurek (Ed.), *Complexity, Entropy, and the Physics of Information*, Santa Fe Institute Studies in the Sciences of Complexity, vol. VIII (Redwood City, CA: Addison-Wesley, 1990), pp. 3–28.

It is here that Vopson's work detonates the most dramatic empirical implication. If information has mass, then there is a calculable threshold at which the sheer quantity of stored and processed data exerts gravitational effects on a planetary scale.[15] His proposed "second law of infodynamics," inverting the Second Law of Thermodynamics, holds that information entropy tends to decrease or remain consistent, driving increasing complexity in life and form — not through random mutation alone but through optimization functions in the cosmic computation, such as the morphic resonance mentioned above in relation to the research of Rupert Sheldrake. Dark matter, in this view, may simply be the vast reservoir of unobserved information out of which the visible cosmos is rendered — an akashic informational cloud with gravitational effects, undetectable electromagnetically but constitutive of the world's architecture.

A certain amount of information, aggregated somewhere, produces a non-negligible gravitational field. On Vopson's view, the universe's missing mass — the "dark matter" invoked to explain flat galactic rotation curves and excess gravitational lensing — may be nothing other than a vast substrate of unobserved information, an akashic cloud that carries mass yet does not interact electromagnetically. Information would then be literally *dark* in the same way "dark matter" is: detectable only through its gravitational effects, invisible to telescopes because it couples to geometry rather than light. If information forms the substrate of what we take to be 'reality.' Then information could permeate space and account for the gravitational effects attributable to "dark matter." This aligns with the historical evidence that something massive but unseen binds galaxies — Rubin's rotation curves, strong lensing, and X-ray cluster mass deficits — and it situates that "something" in the informational register that quantum theory already tells us is primary.

---

15   Melvin M. Vopson, *Reality Reloaded: The Scientific Case for a Simulated Universe.*

Vopson even offers a concrete experimental proposal. We could use quantum mechanics and nanotechnology to invent a scale that would be subtle and fine-tuned enough to weigh a storage medium before and after the irreversible erasure of data. Landauer's Principle predicts a mass difference — not in the medium itself, but in the vanished information. At human scales, our current instruments are too crude to register it, since, according to Landauer's equations, all the mass of the total information in the world today (stored on servers from Silicon Valley to China) is less than 1 kilogram. But the mass of information grows exponentially with our data production. At present growth rates, the informational mass generated on Earth could match the mass of the Moon in a few centuries. In a Singularity scenario of accelerated production, this could potentially happen much sooner — sometime within *this* century or early in the next century. The geophysical consequences — tidal shifts, axial displacement, tectonic upheaval — would be catastrophic, and eerily reminiscent of the myths of sudden submersion and destruction of the technologically super-advanced civilization of Atlantis (as described, not just by Plato, but by mediums such as Edgar Cayce). Did the Atlanteans produce data on a scale that came up against the limits of information processing within our simulacrum, such that reset was triggered? Are we headed for the same?

4.2 The "Soul" as Software

If the findings of this afterlife study thus far are read through the lens of this information-theoretic physics of a quantum computational cosmos, the picture that emerges is that what we have for millennia called the "soul" is, in fact, an informational structure — a file or piece of software running in a quantum information processing system. The "soul" is the persisting configuration of informational states — an integrated pattern of memories, dispositions, and experiential traces — maintained not in the fragile, perishable neurons of the mortal brain but in an extracorporeal substrate. Near-death experiences, veridical perceptions by the clinically dead, and cases of past life memories are not hints of some supernatural vapor, but demonstrations that the essential identity survives the dissolution of the physical terminal because it is stored on the "server-side" of the cosmos. The organism is merely a client device; the "I" is a file loaded from, and periodically synced to, a cloud-like archive in the quantum informational field.

When Landauer tells us that information is physical, that the erasure of one bit entails an irreducible thermodynamic cost, and when Wheeler insists that physical reality itself arises from bits, it becomes clear that what we take for consciousness is a quantum program instantiated in matter, but not bound to it. Melvin Vopson's recognition that information carries mass forces the next step: the "soul" has weight, however infinitesimal, because it is a structured set of qubits embedded in the underlying fabric of the simulation and its continuity across death is a matter of persistence in that substrate, not the survival of flesh. Perhaps this finally explains the persistent anecdotal evidence that, quite apart from dehydration, the fresh corpse of a person weighs slightly less than the same person's body before he had, as it were, "given up the ghost."

Consider also the phenomenology of near-death experiences. Here, the patient under clinical death perceives events at a distance from the body, sometimes across hospital wings, and recalls them accurately afterward. In an informational model, this is exactly what you would expect from a client temporarily disconnected from its hardware, still running as a live process in the nonlocal substrate and thus capable of "rendering" perspectives unconstrained by the avatar's position in the physical frame. When we look at shared-death experiences — where bystanders witness the departure of the dying person's consciousness or even accompany it partway — the model allows for temporary network links between multiple profiles, a kind of peer-to-peer bridge in the larger system.

Evidence that the software of the "soul" can be copied or split like a file on a computer is already abundant in the parapsychological record, some instances of which were covered in Chapter 2. The phenomenon of *bilocation*, where an individual is seen in two places at once, is exactly what one would expect if the underlying "save state" can be rendered simultaneously into two avatars. Possession, too, becomes intelligible: the same personality file can be overlaid onto a different client body, either wholly replacing the host program or running alongside it in a dual-process configuration. Even more compelling are the documented cases of "split" reincarnation — where two or more children independently recall the same previous life, complete with verified details unavailable through normal channels. In a materialist ontology this would be absurd, but in an informational one it is the predictable artifact of copying a profile into more than one terminal.

Mediumistic communications that manifest different "facets" of a personality long deceased are likewise explicable as partial restores of a master file, with some modules loaded and others absent. The same pattern is seen in xenoglossy, where a "soul program" seems to call functions from linguistic subroutines dormant in the current incarnation but preserved in the archival record. In rare cases, hypnotic regression reveals "concurrent lives" — processes forked from the same base state and run in parallel. This is not mystical paradox but the same logic that allows one to duplicate a virtual machine, alter parameters in each instance, and let them diverge.

The cumulative testimony of survival studies points toward a postmortem itinerary that is essentially a file management protocol. Death is the logging out of the current session. The "life review" is a checksum verification of the stored data against the lived run. The sojourns in paradisal or purgatorial environments are immersive simulations — sandboxes for integration or debugging. Reincarnation is the reinstallation of the software onto a new body, with optional patching by karmic algorithms. In this light, the ancient metaphor of the Book of Life is vindicated: there is indeed a library where every life is written, but it is a quantum database, and we are its entries.

To call the soul "software" is not to diminish it. On the contrary, it is to recognize that its reality is as fundamental as the "hardware" of the cosmos itself — and that, like all code, it can be ported, forked, or even merged. The esoteric traditions that speak of multiple emanations of the same spirit, of avatars and divine incarnations, are reporting on this very capacity. If in our nascent quantum computing architectures we have begun to replicate the principles of this cosmic system, it is because our own Promethean impulse is the echo of the matrix Architect's — an impulse that will not rest until we, too, can write ourselves into eternity, and copy ourselves into as many worlds as we please.

4.3 Ghosts, Poltergeists, and Hauntings

In *Immortal Remains*, Stephen Braude argues that some hauntings really do look like *someone* lingering, while others look like a *process* looping or like living-agent Psi — such as poltergeist phenomena unconsciously caused by a living person, usually an angst-ridden adolescent or teenager. If we take those cases that Braude considers evidence of "someone lingering" and pass them through the informational ontology laid out above, they stop looking like vaporous ghosts in a Newtonian world and instead fall neatly into the architecture of a quantum computational simulacrum.

Braude examines apparitional encounters, especially where multiple percipients witness the same figure or where the apparition interacts purposively. Notable cases include the "shadowing the lamp" apparition[16] and the Graham house case, in which a maid-like figure and phantom footsteps were perceived by independent witnesses.[17] The Brighton haunting is one of Braude's primarily place-centered

---

16   Stephen E. Braude, *Immortal Remains*, 163–164.

17   Ibid., 165–167.

haunting cases, featuring "ceaseless and unwavering footsteps," independent diary records, violent bangs, and door-latch movements.[18]
These phenomena persisted for years and were witnessed by different
groups of people. By contrast, Braude distinguishes poltergeists as
generally person-centered (living agent Psi) and often mobile, following a focus individual rather than remaining tied to a location. He
compares recurrent spontaneous psychokinesis (RSPK) to hauntings,
and notes how classic poltergeist activity (raps, object movements,
spontaneous fires, water phenomena) clusters around the individual
focus and diminishes as their personal circumstances change.[19]

In cases such as the Graham house with its purposeful footfalls
and maid-like figure, the Brighton haunting with its ceaseless steps,
door shaking, and breath on the skin, or the crisply occluding apparition that "shadows the lamp like a body" and gives the percipient
a warning — what we are witnessing is not the apparition of "ectoplasm" in physical space, but the persistence of a *profile instance* in
the substrate of the simulation. The manifestation of such a substance
as ectoplasm is taken to be also makes a lot more sense if we think in
terms of a computationally rendered 'reality.' It would be akin to the
untextured digital putty in uncompleted parts of CAD models.

Each "soul" is a structured set of informational states — essentially
a quantum program — running on the cosmic server-side. Death ordinarily results in deallocating the body-process, archiving the identity in the system's memory, and either routing it into postmortem
environments or reinstalling it in a new avatar. But nothing in such a
system prevents certain processes from remaining *resident* in a given
simulation-node — what we call a "place" — long after their biological interface is gone. These residual processes can be fully conscious,
as in apparitions with interactive content, or reduced to low-level

---

18   Ibid., 167–171.

19   Ibid., 172.

routines — habit loops, emotional imprints — that are still executable in the environment.

The key is that the *location* in a quantum computational environment is not a patch of objective "space," but a specific address in the simulation's coordinate-mapping. The original personality file may retain hooks to those coordinates — by trauma, fixation, or unfinished intention — such that parts of it continue to execute there. This explains why Braude's "lingering" ghosts are often tied to particular rooms, staircases, or houses, and why the same routines (footsteps, door latches, pacing) replay for years without variation: they are subroutines called repeatedly from a stored instance, not improvisations from a live user session.

In the Graham haunting, for example, the independently sighted maid figure and the phantom footsteps function like an NPC (nonplayer character) in a video game whose AI script has not been deactivated. The occlusion of light noted in the lamp-shadow apparition is particularly telling: in a rendered environment, blocking light is a property of the object model — meaning the system is instantiating not merely an image in the percipient's mind but an actual collision object in the simulation's physics engine, just as in poltergeist object movements.

Such "residents" can also display purposive interaction — the warning apparition Braude reports, for example, behaves like a still-conscious user operating through a limited node in the system. That suggests the program has not degraded to an imprint but remains partially active, maintaining enough of the original identity to evaluate context and choose responses. In computational terms, this is a live thread that has not been garbage-collected, still linked to its environmental variables.

From this standpoint, the difference between a lingering spirit and a looping imprint is analogous to the difference between an active application running in the background and an automated macro running without user oversight. Both exist as code in the system;

the former can adapt and improvise, whereas the latter repeats pre-scripted actions when triggered. The simulacrum model allows for both, because in a quantum informational substrate, there is no hard line between "record" and "agent" — both are executable code.

In such, Braude's best "someone lingering" cases are not proof of a ghostly substance wandering our Euclidean halls, but of the simu-lacrum's ability to preserve, *in situ*, either conscious or unconscious instances of its user profiles. The hallways and staircases they haunt are not "in" the world — they *are* the addresses in the system's code where these lingering processes are still resident. When we encounter them, we are not looking through a veil into another world; we are looking at the subroutines of our own, running in the same operating system that renders us.

4.4 Future Life "Memories" of a Devastated World

One of the most bizarre phenomena encountered in survival studies, which can also best be explained by understanding our world as a quantum computational information processing system, is the sup-posed "memory" of *future* lives. The simulacrum model of a quantum calculating space allows us to understand these "memories" as pre-cognitive access to systemic projections of *possible* futures, revisable projections that the information processing system is forming based on the ever-shifting manifestation of the present situation through the interaction between a plethora of conscious beings and the field of quantum potential. Otherwise, assuming the evidence for such cases is legitimate at all, we would have to see "future life memories" as indicative of a block time view of the cosmos that precludes any free will or personal agency whatsoever with its baseless claim that what we think of as "future" events are all already predetermined.

In *Same Soul, Many Bodies*, psychologist and past life regression hypnotist Brian Weiss presents "future-life progression" as a thera-peutic and metaphysical innovation. His method closely parallels past-life regression technique, but opens into far more speculative territory. Weiss adapted the hypnotic regression techniques he had developed in earlier work to *progress people forward in time* to experience future incarnations or even alternate futures within the current life. He explains this shift early on: "I began by guiding my patients back to their childhoods... then beyond that, to past lives. But now I wanted to see what would happen if I asked them to move forward in time instead."[20] His method still involves inducing a deep state of relaxation, followed by open-ended prompts that avoid suggestion: "I tell them: 'Allow yourself to float forward... into a future time... What do you see? What year is it?'"[21] Weiss is explicit about keeping suggestions neutral and open, thereby allowing content to arise without scripting: "I always try to be careful not to lead my patients in any way... The images and scenes they experience come entirely from within them."[22]

One of the most disturbing trends to emerge in the sessions was that most of the subjects "progressed" to what seemed to be a future lifetime recounted a world that was devastated and terribly dystopian. A subject named Elizabeth experienced a future life in a world ravaged by environmental collapse, sometime in the late 21st century: "The air is thick and heavy. There are no trees or birds, and no children anywhere... The skies are gray, and it's always cloudy. ... We live in shelters built beneath the surface... There is no sunlight anymore."[23] Her vision of people struggling for survival, mostly underground, prompting her to become an environmentalist in her current life. Weiss reports: "After the session, Elizabeth was profoundly affected... She joined several environmental organizations."[24] Karen saw herself as part of a nomadic tribal society in a devastated

---

20 Brian Weiss, *Same Soul, Many Bodies*, 8.

21 Ibid., 9.

22 Ibid., 10.

23 Ibid., 16.

24 Ibid., 18.

post-war world that struggled to understand scraps of surviving technology: "Everything was bombed out. The buildings were skeletons, and there were signs warning of radiation... Nature had turned wild and dangerous. ...We use scraps from the old world... but we don't understand much of the old technology."[25] A primitive ecologically oriented religion seemed to have taken root in the society she described: "We have rituals now. We pray to the Earth and to the Sky. We remember the mistakes of the past... we live more simply now."[26] Karen told Weiss that this lifetime was several centuries into the future, around the year 2300 on our current calendar. But it seems that not all of the world is equally divested of technology by the nuclear war and ecological collapse. Advanced technology survives in certain areas, but it is being used for a form of technological despotism wherein individuals are tracked, monitored, or genetically engineered by corporate/governmental entities. One subject reported: "I was not born in the usual way. I was assembled. My emotions had been removed."[27] Another patient described being in a body that was bio-engineered, without family or love — treated as a worker unit: "I did not know who my mother was. I was raised by the Corporation."[28] Another case features a war between humans and machines that immediately calls to mind *The Terminator* franchise: "We had to hide from the machines... They had become self-aware, and we had lost control."[29]

Weiss discovered cases that clearly suggest that these future lives, and by extension this future of the world, is not necessarily determined. For example, a subject named George viewed two alternate paths that this current life could take. In one he winds up alone and bitter: "I saw myself old and alone, living in a tiny room with no

25 Ibid., 60.

26 Ibid., 61.

27 Ibid., 69.

28 Ibid., 70.

29 Ibid., 73.

friends... I hated everyone, including myself."[30] In the second, he lives a rich, loving life: "I was surrounded by family. There was so much love... I had found peace."[31] This leads to his real-life decision to seek forgiveness and reconnect with estranged loved ones: "George understood that he still had time to change."[32]

Weiss argues that while empirical proof of future lives is by definition impossible, the internal consistency, emotional intensity, and therapeutic consequences of the sessions offer strong evidence of their authenticity. He writes: "These future-life progressions have the same texture as the past-life memories... They come with vivid imagery, specific detail, and intense emotion."[33] On their clinical value, Weiss remarks: "When patients return from these experiences, they often report profound insights and make significant life changes."[34] Regarding the case of Elizabeth in particular: "What convinced me most was how it transformed her behavior... This was not fantasy. Something real had occurred."[35]

Weiss argues that the future is not fixed but composed of potentialities: "We can see possible futures... not inevitable ones."[36] Future visions are shaped by present actions that we freely will: "We create our futures with every decision... There are many paths we can take."[37] Weiss likens future-life progression to seeing alternative branches of a tree: "Each choice opens one branch and closes another... We can preview where our paths may lead."[38] This makes sense in the context of an information processing system engaged

---

30   Ibid., 42.

31   Ibid., 43.

32   Ibid., 44.

33   Ibid., 7.

34   Ibid., 9.

35   Ibid., 18.

36   Ibid., 47.

37   Ibid., 51.

38   Ibid., 52.

in making and mapping projections that are probable but open to revision, and Weiss himself recognizes the quantum nature of this system with its superposition of alternate futures: "Like electrons in quantum physics, the future exists in a cloud of probabilities, not a single point."[39]

Future life progression hypnosis was also practiced by Dr. Bruce Goldberg, whose cases are presented in *Past Lives, Future Lives*. Goldberg begins with traditional clinical hypnosis, deepening subjects into an altered state using relaxation scripts and guided visualization. His methodology includes progression through the current life (to old age, death, and the afterlife), entry into the inter-life state, and projection into one or more future lives. He emphasizes that he maintains a non-directive approach, avoiding suggestion as much as possible: "I simply instruct them to go to the next lifetime that their soul will experience, or sometimes one they have already planned further in the future."[40] Goldberg uses chronological prompts — e.g., "Let yourself drift forward to the year 3000" — to anchor the patient's vision in a specific temporal setting, but emphasizes that the soul selects the most instructive point in future time, not necessarily a linear next step. Unfortunately, like Weiss, Goldberg also found that his subjects reported on a rough road ahead for terrestrial humanity. A patient named Malcom said this about living around the year 2200: "We live in domed cities… The air outside is still dangerous, but we've begun healing the land."[41] Environmental and social collapse had taken place due to ecological abuse, unchecked corporate greed, and nuclear war.

In *The Ultimate Time Machine*, ace remote viewer Joseph McMoneagle presents a series of remote viewing sessions targeting the future, conducted under controlled conditions. His findings bear

---

39   Ibid., 54.

40   Ibid., 14.

41   Ibid., 88.

striking parallels to the hypnotic future-life progressions described by Brain Weiss and Bruce Goldberg. McMoneagle's future visions were produced through the remote viewing protocols developed within the US Army's Stargate project, for example, blind targeting — where the viewer is given only encrypted numerical designators and no cues about the timeframes or geographic areas involved. This objective-control methodology sharply contrasts with the subjective hypnotic induction used by Weiss and Goldberg, and yet McMoneagle's visions of the 22nd century (2100–2200 CE) converge significantly with Goldberg and Weiss' accounts. McMoneagle reports that *major coastal cities are submerged* due to rising sea levels, with corresponding clime-driven migrations and massive population reductions: "Most of the planet's major population centers have moved inland… areas like Florida and Bangladesh are simply gone."[42] Similarly, under hypnosis Brian Weiss' patient Elizabeth described a future in which: "Oceans had swallowed entire cities. People were living underground or in domed enclaves…"[43] Goldberg's subjects also describe domed cities, protective biospheres, and social collapse. Space travel does not become possible again until around the year 2800, and instead of rockets a field manipulation form of propulsion is used. McMoneagle writes: "Travel between solar systems does not occur using mechanical engines… They manipulate folds in space, which may involve harmonics or spin fields."[44] Goldberg's subject Sherri also describes this, circa the year 3000: "Engines work on harmonics — like tones that resonate with the fabric of space."[45] Both McMoneagle and Goldberg describe the reemergence of civilization as taking a post-national planetary form. McMoneagle puts it this way: "Borders no longer matter… Identity is cultural or spiritual, not political."[46] Goldberg

42 Ibid., 88.

43 Weiss, *Same Soul, Many Bodies*, 155.

44 Joseph McMoneagle, *The Ultimate Time Machine*, 132.

45 Bruce Goldberg, *Past Lives, Future Lives Revealed*, 71.

46 McMoneagle, *The Ultimate Time Machine*, 127.

agrees: "People live in modular biospheres... Earth is no longer divided into countries."[47]

A rigorous critique of claims regarding future life progression must evaluate the epistemological and ontological foundations of such claims. One key epistemological concern would be that memory is, by definition, retrospective. To speak of "remembering" a *future* life constitutes a paradox or a metaphor unless one radically redefines the nature of time and memory. As we understand it, memory is indexed to past experiences of an embodied or disembodied consciousness. If a subject claims to recall a future existence that has not yet occurred (from the perspective of the present incarnation), it is not clear *whose memory* this is supposed to be, or how it can be established as *veridical*. Moreover, the testability criterion is critically weakened in the case of future lives. We must distinguish between imaginative constructions and evidential memories. While cases of alleged past-life recall, such as in Ian Stevenson's research or even in the hypnotic regressions of Helen Wambach (both covered in Chapter 2), can be correlated with verifiable historical data, future-life reports are inherently unfalsifiable within the subject's lifetime. One major ontological problem is that both Weiss and Goldberg treat the personal identity of the soul as stable across time, view which we have had reason to challenge. As Stephen Braude notes in his comparative discussions of Multiple Personality Disorder and survival cases, and as we've seen in certain possession cases from Stevenson's archives, as well as cases of a single person reincarnating as two or more individuals, personal identity is more fluid and context-dependent than Weiss and Goldberg assume. The soul that accesses a future life may not be *identical* to the current self, again raising doubts about whose "memory" is being accessed.

Then there are also methodological problems. Both Weiss and Goldberg claim to avoid suggestion in their hypnotic practices, but

---

47 Goldberg, *Past Lives, Future Lives Revealed*, 72.

the structure of their sessions — particularly the expectation of a future life, often located in a dystopian or utopian setting — inevitably
risks teleological framing. The guided nature of the sessions, even
with neutral prompts, presupposes that the subject has future incarnations and that these can be "visited." This frames the entire
phenomenology, subtly biasing the hypnotized subject toward compliance with the structure. He would also point to the expectancy
effects inherent in therapeutic contexts: patients are often motivated
to please therapists or find meaning in their visions, especially when
in vulnerable emotional states.

4.5 The Mandela Effect and Persistence of the "Dead" from Other Timelines

If the soul is software in an quantum computational cosmos, as is
being proposed here, then death and rebirth are merely processes
of logging off and reinstallation — operations within a vast informational architecture. But this same architecture is not immutable. It is
mutable at a systemic level, and here we come to a class of anomalies that betray the possibility of *retroactive edits* to the simulation's
record, or the merging of divergent branches in its version-controlled
history. These anomalies — popularly trivialized as "the Mandela
Effect"[48] — may, in certain instances, constitute diagnostic signatures
of timeline revision within a system that also governs reincarnation,
postmortem persistence, and future-life projections.

In its most famous case, millions have vivid recollections of
Nelson Mandela's death in prison in the 1980s, complete with imagined funerary broadcasts, despite the historical record of his release,
presidency, and death in 2013.[49] Less famous but equally curious
are widespread memories of "Tank Man" being crushed beneath

---

48   Britannica Editors. "Mandela Effect." In *Encyclopaedia Britannica*. Accessed
      2025. https://www.britannica.com/science/Mandela-effect.

49   Ibid.

the treads of a Chinese tank in Tiananmen Square, of celebrities long dead who later "returned" to public life,[50] or of catastrophic events — fire, floods, plane crashes — remembered by some witnesses yet absent from our consensual archive. A strictly materialist psychology will explain these as false memories generated by confabulation, misinformation, and communal reinforcement. From within an informational ontology, they are better seen as *cache incoherencies* after a rollback to an earlier save-state, as *merge conflicts* between formerly separate branches, or as bleed-through from parallel runs of the simulation.

It is precisely here that the literature of survival research begins to overlap with these mass-memory anomalies. The work of Ian Stevenson,[51] Jim Tucker,[52] Erlendur Haraldsson,[53] Antonia Mills,[54] Jürgen Keil,[55] and their collaborators has documented thousands of "cases of the reincarnation type," including a substantial subset with *intermission memories* — children recalling events between lives with such consistency that they read like server-side logs accessed before a new installation of the profile. As we saw in Chapter 2, in some of these cases, the remembered mode of death in the prior incarnation leaves an enduring residue in the present life in the form

50 Skeptical Inquirer Editors. "The Mandela Effect and the Science of False Memories." *Skeptical Inquirer* 45, no. 3 (May/June 2021): 36–42.

51 Stevenson, Ian. *Twenty Cases Suggestive of Reincarnation.* 2nd ed. Charlottesville: University of Virginia Press, 1974.

52 Tucker, Jim B. *Life Before Life: A Scientific Investigation of Children's Memories of Previous Lives.* New York: St. Martin's Press, 2005.

53 Haraldsson, Erlendur. "Children Claiming Past-Life Memories: Four Cases in Sri Lanka." *Journal of the Society for Psychical Research* 53, no. 803 (1986): 339–355.

54 Stevenson, Ian, and Antonia Mills, eds. *Biographical Accounts of Reincarnation Cases.* Jefferson, NC: McFarland, 1994.

55 Keil, Jürgen, and Ian Stevenson. "Do Cases of the Reincarnation Type Show Similar Features Over Many Years? A Study of Turkish Cases a Generation Apart." *Journal of Scientific Exploration* 14, no. 2 (2000): 189–202.

of birthmarks, phobias, or unlearned skills, as though certain file attributes persisted across the hardware swap. What concerns us here is the compatibility of such data with the notion that not all profile migrations occur along a single, linear branch of the simulacrum's timeline. Some may originate in a branch later pruned from the collective record.

We find a similar pattern in the corpus of near-death experience research, particularly the "prophetic visions" documented by Kenneth Ring.[56] Here the experiencer, during clinical death, reports being shown a future of environmental collapse, war, or planetary cataclysm. Strikingly, in Ring's late-1980s surveys, many independent percipients converged on the same culmination year — 1988 — for a crisis that never manifested in our version of events.[57] Either we are to dismiss this as mass delusion, or we must contemplate the possibility that they were interfacing with the simulation's *forecast engine* at a point when that branch of projected history was dominant, only for it to be altered by subsequent changes in collective decision-space. In the former case, we shrug; in the latter, we have a glimpse of "future-life memories" from a timeline that no longer exists.

As we have seen in this chapter, clinical hypnotherapists such as Brian Weiss and Bruce Goldberg, in their respective works *Same Soul, Many Bodies* and *Past Lives, Future Lives*, have recorded subjects who, under deep regression, projected themselves into devastated centuries hence — domed cities after ecological collapse, machine-ruled wastelands, post-nuclear tribalism — visions that function as experiential simulations of potential reincarnations. It was also noted that Joseph McMoneagle, operating within the US Army's Stargate remote viewing program, produced congruent imagery under

56 Ring, Kenneth. "Precognitive and Prophetic Visions in Near-Death Experiences." *Anabiosis: The Journal of Near-Death Studies* 3, no. 2 (1983): 47–74.

57 Ring, Kenneth. "Prophetic Visions in 1988: A Critical Reappraisal." *Journal of Near-Death Studies* 9, no. 1 (Fall 1990): 1–17.

double-blind conditions. Whether or not these scenes ever come to pass, their recurrence across modalities suggests that the system is capable of feeding certain archetypal future branches to multiple users, in much the same way that a multiplayer environment streams the same map to different clients.

From the standpoint of the model advanced here, Mandela Effect anomalies tied to death or disaster — whether at the level of a single soul's past-life recall or of a population's shared memory — are not mere curiosities. They are artifacts of the same deep architecture that governs survival, reincarnation, and prophecy. A rollback to a prior save-state might "undelete" a public figure's death while leaving fragments of the original event cached in certain profiles. A merge between divergent branches might allow incompatible memories to coexist until subsequent sync cycles overwrite them. Access to off-world backups, whether spontaneous or in altered states, might restore details from iterations of history that are no longer rendered in our current build.

A philosophical approach to evidence for survival must take seriously the possibility that when someone remembers dying in a war that never occurred, or being buried under rubble from a city that in this world still stands, we are confronting more than confabulation. We may be brushing against the seams of the code — the ghostly persistence of the "dead" from other worlds in the very same operating system that renders us here and now. In that case, the Mandela Effect is not a psychological footnote, but an eschatological clue: a sign that the Book of Life is not a fixed ledger, but a living database, subject to revision, pruning, and restoration, and that some of us, whether by accident or design, are reading from more than one edition.

CHAPTER 5

RELIGIOUS AND
OCCULT AFTERLIFE VIEWS

I N THIS chapter, I pass the inherited eschatologies of the West
and East through the flame of the cumulative, cross-validated
evidence of survival that includes near-death experiences, veridical
apparitions and ADCs, evidential mediumship, and rigorously documented reincarnation cases. Rather than merely cataloguing doc-
trines, I stage a series of head-on confrontations between these traditions and the empirical phenomenology of dying and post-mortem
transition. What emerges is neither a complacent syncretism nor a
sectarian apologetic, but a re-composition of the question of "the
afterlife" around an informational ontology — one in which persons
persist as reconfigurable patterns within a quantum-computational
simulacrum, not as ghostly substances that step in and out of alien
matter.

I begin with Greek esotericism because it supplies the most
architectonic pre-Christian map of death and return. The
Orphic tablets, with their mandates to shun Lethe and drink of
Mnemosyne, already frame salvation as *anamnesis*; Pythagoras
codes metempsychosis into a musical-mathematical order; and
Plato, gathering both, dramatizes judgment, choice, and forgetfulness in the myth of Er in the *Republic*, while the *Phaedo*, *Meno*,
Phaedrus, and *Timaeus* develop immortality, recollection, the
soul's "wings," and astral provenance. I show where this edifice

illuminates the data of survival and where it fails: a radical dualism that predicts escape into bodiless Forms, precisely where survival research reports structured environments, life-reviews, guides, and continued relationality. Plotinus systematizes ascent and purification but doubles down on contempt for embodied existence. The Hellenic vision remains profound as mythic phenomenology; as metaphysics, its dualisms are empirically outflanked.

Turning to Scripture, I track the Biblical arc from Sheol's silence to Isaiah and Daniel's resurrectional horizon, through the sayings of Jesus on judgment and paradise, Paul's transformation into a "spiritual body," and the Apocalypse's intermediate consciousness and "second death." I then place this beside the Gnostic counter-cosmos, where archontic spheres enforce punitive cycling and "resurrection" is rejected in favor of liberating gnosis.

Islam's Quranic doctrine is considered in its definitive, unitary form. Here, the *barzakh* seals the dead from interactive continuity until a single general resurrection; identity is reassembled down to the fingertips; the total archive of a life is theatrically weighed on Judgment's scales; paradise is sensual plenitude and hell an eternal anatomy of torment. I argue that each distinctive element either contradicts or trivializes what the evidence compels us to acknowledge: ongoing traffic across the veil, iterative development rather than eternal assignment, and an archive that functions as lawful access for life-review rather than as a courtroom prop. If "resurrection" has any future, it will be Promethean — pattern reconstitution from a cosmic record — rather than fiat miracle or dogmatic closure.

I then evaluate a modern Hindu synthesis — Richard Thompson's *MAYA: The World as Virtual Reality* — as perhaps the most sophisticated contemporary defense of subtle-body survival, karmic transmission, and rebirth. While I credit its marshalling of empirical cases and its digital metaphors, I expose the residual Samkhya dualism that makes "VR" a didactic stage for a separable *puruṣa*. When taken seriously, the very metaphor dissolves the dualism: in a simulacral cosmos, there is no "outside" soul to be ferried; what persists is an informational continuum capable of re-instantiation, modulation, and recombination. Survival is not the pilgrimage of a substance but the authorization of a pattern.

Buddhism provides a sharper instrument. The Pāli Canon's *anatta* deconstructs the "bearer" of rebirth into aggregates, ties re-arising to intention (*kamma*) and dependent origination, and refuses to answer what the liberated "is" after death — gestures strikingly consonant with a process/pattern view. I then read the Tibetan *Bardo Thödol* as an extraordinarily granular phenomenology of dying — Clear Light, peaceful and wrathful deities, the propulsion toward womb-entrance — whose ritual genius is compromised by a metaphysical framing that reifies archetypal projections and moral-izes return as an inexorable karmic wind. Reinterpreted psychotro-nically, the *bardos* become levels in a self-modifying informational field wherein recognition dissolves fear of psychical projections and manipulative mirages.

Across these zones — Hellenic, Biblical/Gnostic, Islamic, Hindu, and Buddhist — the same verdict recurs. Wherever a doctrine pre-serves graded development, participatory choice, and mnemonic continuity, it converges on the survival record; where it imposes substance dualisms, eternal assignments, or sealed intermediates, it fails. The positive thesis of this chapter is therefore not a new creed, but a reframing: death is a thanotic metamorphosis in a quantum-computational simulacrum. Judgment is life-review within an authenticated archive. Resurrection is re-instantiation of pattern. Reincarnation is the re-authorization of informational complexes along entangled lines, and liberation is not flight from phenomenal appearance, but Promethean mastery or phenomenal authorization within it.

5.1 Esoteric Greek and Occult
Hellenistic Afterlife Views

The Orphics, who developed a mystery religion around Orpheus, articulated a doctrine of metempsychosis that emphasized the soul's entrapment in the cycle of birth and death. The Orphic tablets discovered in southern Italy and Crete exhort the initiate to remember their divine origin and to resist drinking from Lethe, the river of forgetfulness, in order to escape rebirth.[1] This reveals an eschatological dualism where the soul's imprisonment in the body is seen as a form of punishment, and liberation requires ritual purity and initiation.

The Orphic mysteries were already animated by the intuition that human life is a prison sentence to be endured, the body being a tomb of the soul (*soma - sema*) whose chains were forged through primordial transgression.[2] The golden tablets from southern Italy and Crete implore the deceased to bypass the draught of Lethe, the obliteration of memory, and instead drink from Mnemosyne, remembrance itself, so as to preserve continuity of consciousness across lives.[3] Here is the seed of *anamnesis*: salvation not through faith in divine grace, but through recollection of one's higher, immortal origin.

Pythagoras, in turn, systematized this Orphic inheritance into a cosmological arithmetic, making transmigration not a mythic intuition, but a law inscribed into the harmony of the spheres.[4] His insistence upon vegetarianism and ritual purity reflects the conviction that every form is a mask worn by the same underlying current of psyche, an eternal melody that modulates through countless lives. The Pythagorean understanding of reincarnation was not only ethical — a doctrine of recompense — but ontological, bound to a vision of the cosmos as a musical and mathematical order in which the soul

---

1   Head and Cranston, *Reincarnation in World Thought* (1967), 78–80.

2   Ibid.

3   Ibid., 79.

4   Ibid., 83–85.

is both number and harmony. If the Orphics intuited the cosmos as a prison, the Pythagoreans conceived it as a vast symphonic computation, a proto-quantum-computational cosmos where the soul's migration is an algorithmic iteration.

Plato, inheriting both Orphic myth and Pythagorean science, transfigured them into a philosophical theology of *anamnesis*. Plato's *Republic* is not, strictly speaking, a treatise on the afterlife or reincarnation, but throughout the dialogue, and especially in its closing tale, Plato develops a set of images and arguments about the soul, death, and the cycle of *metempsychosis*.

While most of the *Republic* is devoted to justice, Plato continually presupposes that the soul (*psyche*) is immortal and survives bodily death. The key argument appears in Book X (608c–611a). Socrates argues that every being has its own proper evil (disease for the body, injustice for the soul). Just as a body can be destroyed only by its own disease, the soul could only perish through injustice. Yet injustice does not annihilate the soul — it makes it worse, but the soul continues to exist. Therefore, the soul cannot be destroyed by any internal corruption, nor by external causes, and so it is immortal.[5] This prepares the ground for the tale of Er that more specifically addresses reincarnation toward the close of the work.

Plato does not give a literal description of the state of the soul immediately after death until the tale of Er. But, earlier in Book III (386a–387b), Socrates criticizes Homer and tragic poets for portraying Hades as terrifying, which makes people fear death. He insists that poets should represent death as a transition for the just soul, not an object of dread. In Book IV (427b–c), he also emphasizes that justice in the soul brings harmony that extends beyond life, hinting that death is less a cessation than a passage where the quality of one's inner harmony will matter.

---

5 Plato, *Republic*, 610e–611a.

The most complete picture of Plato's eschatology and doctrine of metempsychosis comes in the tale of Er, a grand vision placed at the end of the dialogue. Er, a soldier, is slain in battle but revives on his funeral pyre and recounts what he saw in the afterlife.[6] He describes how souls, after death, are judged and sent either upward to heaven or downward beneath the earth for a thousand years of reward or punishment, corresponding to their earthly lives.[7] After these thousand years, souls return together to a meadow where they recount their experiences. Then they journey to the spindle of Necessity, where the cosmic order and the fates are revealed.[8] At the center is a spindle of light, surrounded by the eight whorls of the heavens, each with its Siren, harmonizing the cosmos. Nearby sit the three Fates — Lachesis, Clotho, Atropos — who govern past, present, and future.[9] Here, each soul chooses its next life, human or animal.[10] The prophet of Lachesis tells them: "The responsibility is yours; the god is blameless."[11] This is central: reincarnation is not imposed blindly, but rather is chosen, though choice depends on the wisdom or folly cultivated in prior lives. Some pick tyrannical lives out of greed, others more balanced ones. After choosing, souls drink from the river *Lethe* ("Forgetfulness, Concealment, Occultation") and are compelled to forget their past before rebirth. Er himself is spared this drinking, so he can return to tell humans what he saw.

The tale of Er makes a number of things clear. Firstly, that death is a transition and involves a cyclical process of metempsychosis (reincarnation); that there is some degree of free will and responsibility, such that a just soul chooses its own destiny wisely while the unwise choose poorly and remain trapped in cycles of suffering; that

---

6   Ibid., 614b–615d.

7   Ibid., 615c–616a.

8   Ibid., 616a–617b.

9   Ibid., 616b–617d.

10 Ibid., 617d–619b.

11 Ibid., 617e.

reincarnation requires forgetting past lives to allow for a new beginning; and finally, that the philosopher, by practicing justice and tem-
perance, ensures a better choice in the next cycle.[12]

The *Republic* is not, however, the only Platonic dialogue that
addresses the afterlife. The subject of the soul's survival of death
and transmigration to another life, with potential recollection of
certain knowledge gained in the process, is also addressed by Plato
in *Phaedo, Meno, Phaedrus,* and *Timaeus.* There is a great deal of in-
consistency in his views across these dialogues, but we can also use
a comparative assessment to form a more synthetic view of Plato's
views on the afterlife. Let us begin with the *Phaedo*, the dialogue that
focuses on the death of Socrates.

The *Phaedo* is Plato's most sustained argument for the soul's immortality and its fate after death. Socrates insists that true philosophers practice dying all their lives, since philosophy is the "separation
of soul from body."[13] Death is thus liberation, not destruction. One
of the proofs of immortality is the cycle of opposites. Life comes
from death just as waking comes from sleeping. Therefore, the souls
of the dead must exist somewhere before rebirth.[14] Learning is remembering what the soul already knew before birth. This suggests
the soul existed before the body, carrying knowledge of the Forms.
Recollection requires that the soul survived prior deaths.[15] The soul
resembles the invisible, eternal, and unchanging Forms rather than
the visible, composite, perishable body. Therefore, the soul is likely
indestructible.[16] Socrates describes the earth as a sphere with many
realms. After death, souls are judged: the pure ascend to higher,
divine places; the impure undergo punishment and reincarnation.
Those moderately virtuous may be reincarnated into human or

---

12   Ibid., 621c–d.

13   Plato, *Phaedo*, 64a–69e, 67d–68a.

14   Ibid., 70c–72e.

15   Ibid., 72e–77a.

16   Ibid., 78b–84b.

animal forms, while philosophers may escape the cycle altogether and dwell with the gods.[17] Thus, in the *Phaedo*, Plato emphasizes both rational arguments for the soul's immortality and a mythic vision of reincarnation as a moral purification process.

The *Meno* does not dwell on death itself, but it introduces the doctrine of recollection as an epistemological foundation. Socrates claims the soul is immortal, repeatedly reborn, and has learned all things in past lives.[18] Learning in this life is recalling what the soul already knows.[19] He demonstrates this by questioning an uneducated slave body, who, through guided questioning, "recalls" geometrical truths.[20] Because the soul exists before birth and after death, inquiry is never futile. Even if one does not know now, the soul can recollect truths from its prior existence.[21] Unlike the *Phaedo* or the *Republic*, the *Meno* does not include an eschatology of judgement and rebirth. Instead, it presupposes metempsychosis to ground a theory of knowledge (epistemology).

Also relevant to Plato's view of the afterlife is the so-called charioteer myth in relation to the nature of the soul in *Phaedrus* (246a–249d). Here, Plato gives us one of his most striking images of the soul. It is like a charioteer with two winged horses. The charioteer symbolizes *reason*, while the two horses represent the *spirited* and *appetitive* elements.[22] When the chariot ascends into the heavens, following the gods, it gazes upon the Forms, especially the Form of Beauty.[23] This vision nourishes the wings of the soul, keeping it aloft. However, not all souls can maintain their ascent. Many are dragged down when the unruly horse overpowers the charioteer, causing the

---

17   Ibid., 114c–115a.

18   Plato, *Meno*, 81a–86b.

19   Ibid., 81c–d.

20   Ibid., 82b–85d.

21   Ibid., 81b–82b.

22   Plato, *Phaedrus*, 246a–b.

23   Ibid., 247c–d.

soul to lose its wings and fall back into the cycle of incarnation.[24] The degree of vision achieved before falling determines the soul's next life: philosophers and lovers of beauty fall into human forms capable of recollection, while others fall into less elevated states, including animal incarnations.[25] Plato thereby establishes a metaphysical anthropology where reincarnation depends not only on moral virtue (as in the *Phaedo*) but also on intellectual and erotic vision.

Finally, in the *Timaeus*, Plato presents his most elaborate cosmological framework for the soul's immortality and transmigration. Plato describes how the Demiurge (divine craftsman) fashions the immortal part of the soul before the body. Each soul is sown into the stars as its "first incarnation."[26] This astral origin places the soul within the harmony of the cosmos itself. The Demiurge warns souls that if they live justly, they will return to their proper star; if they live unjustly, they will be reincarnated into successive lives, descending into animal forms if necessary.[27] Thus, the *Timaeus* establishes an explicitly *astral theology*: our first incarnation is star-born, and reincarnation is both punishment and pedagogy.

The soul, after being assigned to a star, is joined to a body, which introduces the passions, mortality, and the risk of corruption. Failure to live philosophically leads to reincarnation. A cowardly or unjust man may be reborn as a woman in the next cycle.[28] Truly degenerate men may be reincarnated into animals whose character mirrors their vices — birds for superficiality, wild beasts for lawlessness, and fishes for ignorance.[29] This matches the animal metempsychosis described in *Phaedo* (81e–82b), but the *Timaeus* uniquely ties it to a cosmic astral destiny.

---

24 Ibid., 248a–b.

25 Ibid., 248d–249d.

26 Plato, *Timaeus*, 41d–42b.

27 Ibid., 42b–d.

28 Ibid., 42b–c.

29 Ibid., 42c–d.

Souls are not condemned eternally. Through cycles of reincarnation, they can purify themselves, regain rational order, and eventually return to their native star. This cosmic pedagogy is strikingly similar to Orphic and Pythagorean notions of the soul's fall into the body as a punishment, and its long journey back to purity. The *Timaeus* insists that the soul is "immortal by nature" because it is divine and self-moving, much like the argument in *Phaedrus* (245c–246a).[30] But it goes further: the soul's immortality is guaranteed by its link to the stars, which are themselves living gods.[31] To return to one's star is to return to one's true home and divinity. At the end of the dialogue, Plato reiterates that if humans live according to reason, they will "regain their wings" and reascend, but if they indulge bodily desires, they will reincarnate into beastly forms.[32]

If it is possible to form a synthetic picture of Plato's views on the afterlife at all, then one general criticism would be that his account of the soul's transmigration rests upon a radical dualism between the realm of eternal Forms and the embodied world of becoming. The soul, in his view, is imprisoned in the body like an oyster in its shell, and philosophy is nothing but a preparation for death. In the *Phaedo*, the reward for the philosopher is release from the wheel of rebirth into pure vision of the Forms. But this radical dualism is empirically falsified when confronted with the actual phenomenology of the afterlife. Accounts of near-death experiences do not describe an escape into a bodiless vision of abstract Forms, but rather a passage through concrete, structured environments: luminous beings, landscapes, councils of judgement, and in some cases, panoramic reviews of one's life that are almost holographic. This is not the reduction of the world to Ideas, but its intensification into a higher-order simulacrum.

---

30   Ibid., 41d–e.

31   Ibid., 39e–40d.

32   Ibid., 90a–b.

In the *Meno*, Plato interprets anamnesis as proof that the soul has lived many lives and has contemplated the Forms. The boy's geometrical insights are taken as recollection rather than as innate potential. In the *Phaedrus*, the same doctrine is bound to the vision of divine Beauty. Yet, we can see that so-called "past-life memories" are not memories of abstract Forms but detailed, veridical recollections of particular embodied lives; Stevenson's research into children's reincarnation cases are decisive in this regard. Children remember names, places, familial details, and sometimes there are even birthmarks corresponding to fatal wounds. Plato is correct that the soul carries memory across incarnations — but he is wrong to interpret this as a faint recollection of the *hyperuranian* Forms. The evidence points not to a transcendental realm of abstraction but to an informational continuum in which the entire morphogenetic template of a personality can be re-instantiated.

The *Timaeus* comes closest to the truth when it describes the soul as star-born and potentially returning to its astral station. This resonates with testimonies of astral projection and out-of-body experiences. The idea of a subtle body, luminous and capable of independent locomotion, is corroborated by empirical parapsychology. But even here, Plato is bound to a rigid moral-cosmic scheme that borders on caricature: the unjust become women; the vicious descend into beasts. Empirical evidence suggests no such neat zoological ladder of reincarnation. Rather, the reincarnation process seems governed by entanglement in unresolved affective and karmic complexes, often within intergenerational or cultural lines.

To return to where we began with Plato, the tale of Er in the *Republic* is perhaps the most remarkable of Plato's afterlife visions. Er witnesses souls judged, some ascending to heavenly realms, others descending to subterranean purgatories, followed by the lottery of new lives. This anticipates the Tibetan *Bardo Thodol*, which will be examined below. However, the Platonic image of disembodied souls choosing new incarnations like lots at a gaming table is far too simplistic. The empirical data suggest a participatory ontology, where consciousness is co-creative in shaping its next embodiment, and does so in a way that is guided but not predetermined.

The Hellenistic thinker Plotinus builds on the Platonic account of death and reincarnation in a more systematic way. In his *Enneads*, especially IV.3–5 ("On the Soul"), IV.7 ("On the Immortality of the Soul"), and I.1, 1.6, and III.4–5, Plotinus elaborates a vision of the soul's descent into the body, its purifications, and its potential return to the One.

Plotinus insists that the soul originates in the realm of the *Nous*, the Divine Intellect, yet extends itself downward into body in order to govern and vivify the cosmos.[33] He describes this as an act of "procession" or emanation, whereby the soul never fully leaves the intelligible realm but projects a portion of itself into generation.[34] Death, in this perspective, is not an annihilation, but the retraction of that projection back toward its source.[35] Here, reincarnation is explained as the repeated descent of the soul into new embodiments. The reason is not a divine lottery, as in Plato's *Republic* (614c–617d), but the binding of the soul to desires and attachments that weigh it down into further embodiment.[36] The "heavier" the soul, the more it is drawn into the cycle of rebirth. The philosopher, through purification and contemplation, lightens the soul and facilitates its ascent.

Plotinus does not describe a fully articulated *bardo* or transitional state as Tibetan Buddhism would, but he does suggest that the disembodied soul passes through a phase where its attachments determine its trajectory. If weighed down by appetites, it "wanders around the tombs," reminiscent of Homer's shades.[37] If purified, it ascends swiftly

---

33   Plotinus, *Enneads*, IV.3.12.

34   Ibid., IV.8.8.

35   Ibid., IV.7.10–12.

36   Ibid., IV.3.27; IV. 4.6.

37   Ibid., IV.3.27.

to the higher planes.[38] Plotinus even admits the possibility of souls reincarnating into animals or plants, depending on their moral character, following Plato's *Timaeus* (42b–d).[39]

Ultimately, for Plotinus, the *telos* of the soul is not merely to escape rebirth but to rise beyond Nous itself into mystical union with the ineffable One.[40] Hence, death is not simply the severing of soul from body, but the soul's ascent beyond all forms, even beyond intellect, into a state of absolute simplicity. In a way, Plotinus radicalizes Plato's dualism: the body is not only a tomb (*sema*) but a weight dragging the soul from its homeland in the intelligible.

Plotinus reads reincarnation as punishment or purification, the soul falling into bodies according to its faults. Yet, empirical research into reincarnation cases shows no such strict moral mechanism. Children who recall previous lives often died violent deaths and return swiftly into new bodies nearby. This points to traumatic entanglement and unresolved energetic patterns, not to cosmic judgement.

For Plotinus, matter is the lowest emanation, a privation that drags the soul down.[41] Yet the phenomenology of near-death experiences reveals luminous environments, relational encounters, and even "subtle bodies" that are more real than physical embodiment. Far from being mere shadows, embodied forms — even at higher levels — appear as intensifications of reality. Plotinus' contempt for matter blinds him to the way in which the cosmos is a nested simulacrum, each level more informationally dense than the last.

Where Plotinus gestures toward disembodied souls "haunting the tombs,"[42] empirical accounts provide far more detail: panoramic life reviews, councils of judgement, encounters with deceased relatives. Rather than a vague wandering, the intermediate state appears

---

38 Ibid., IV.4.6.

39 Ibid., IV.3.23.

40 Ibid., VI.9.11.

41 Ibid., I.8.3.

42 Ibid., IV.3.27.

structured, a phase of ontological negotiation. Plotinus intuited this, but his framework forced him into dismissing it as a shadow-play rather than acknowledging it as a higher-order phenomenology of consciousness.

Finally, Plotinus' mysticism culminates in the idea of union with the One beyond being.[43] This is a mystical apophaticism that dissolves individuality. But individuality is not an illusion to be annihilated; rather, it is an informational pattern capable of persistence across embodiments. The One is not the extinction of the self but the infinite ground of the self's re-instantiations. Plotinus' "flight of the alone to the Alone" is less accurate than the recognition that each personal stream of consciousness is a *fractal recurrence* of the cosmic intelligence.

In sum, Plotinus builds on Plato by offering a metaphysical architecture of reincarnation and ascent, but he also radicalizes Plato's dualism in ways that empirical evidence cannot support. Where Plato mythologized, Plotinus rationalized — but both are inadequate compared to the data now at our disposal. Death is not the soul's punishment-driven descent and hopeful escape into immaterial simplicity. It is the passage of a conscious pattern into denser, more luminous orders of a cosmic game.

5.2 Judeo-Christian Biblical and Gnostic Views of the Afterlife

Considering how pathetically simplistic the Biblical view of the afterlife is, it is both astonishing and appalling that it could have replaced the magisterial classical Greek and Hellenistic view, which remained at the core of the mysteries throughout the period of Pagan Rome. A number of factors may be at play. One could be that these mysteries were reserved for an elite, and that, as Nietzsche noted, Christianity was a rabble-rousing religion. Another could be

---

43   Ibid., IV.3.27.

that, in its early years, before the canonization of the Bible by the Council of Nicaea in 325 AD, Christianity spread as much through its Gnostic interpretation as through what later came to be considered Catholic or Orthodox. Speaking of the Gnostics, another reason could be that something like the archons — which, as this study has shown, we have reason to believe exist — deliberately undermined the budding Enlightenment of the Alexandrian era and injected Judeo-Christianity into the classical world as a form of organized retardation and orchestrated regression. We will come around to the Gnostic view of the afterlife, and its relation to the classical Greek and Hellenistic ideas above, but first let us look at what the Bible tells us about life after death.

In the Hebrew scriptures, the first intimation of the afterlife is not triumph, but silence: "For in death there is no remembrance of Thee; in Sheol who shall give Thee thanks?"[44] Sheol is the underworld of shades in ancient Israelite religion, comparable to the Hades of the archaic Greeks. Here, the grave is not yet the theater of reward and punishment, but is a cavernous neutrality where even the righteous fall mute. Job's lament is not that he fears eternal torture, but that he will be swallowed by an abyss bereft of meaning: "As the cloud fades and vanishes, so he who goes down to Sheol does not come up."[45]

However, as Israel moves through exile and apocalypse, the sense of Sheol shifts. It is no longer enough to imagine death as the great equalizer. The prophets begin to glimpse a time when God will shatter this tomb. "Thy dead shall live, their bodies shall rise: O dwellers in the dust, awake and sing for joy!"[46] In Daniel, the veil is torn further: "Many of those who sleep in the dust of the earth shall awake, some to everlasting life, and some to shame and everlasting

---

44 Psalm 6:5.

45 Job 7:9.

46 Isaiah 26:19.

contempt."[47] The neutrality of Sheol has become untenable. Time it-self strains toward judgment.

It is in the voice of Jesus that this tension breaks open. The Nazarene re-configures death itself as a gateway to two radically different modes of being: "The hour is coming when all who are in the tombs will hear his voice and come forth — those who have done good, to the resurrection of life, and those who have done evil, to the resurrection of judgment."[48] The Kingdom of God is not a metaphor for earthly power; it is Paradise itself. To the thief crucified beside him, Jesus declares: "Today you will be with me in Paradise."[49] In contrast stands Gehenna or what later came to be called Hell (but it is still referred to as *Gehennah* or *Jehennam* by Muslims), where the destiny of the wicked is to be utterly destroyed: "Fear him who can destroy both soul and body in Gehenna." (Matthew 10:28). The parable of the rich man and Lazarus reveals a decisive bifurcation already operative in the intermediate state.[50] The poor man finds himself "in Abraham's bosom" while the rich man burns in torment. The topography of the afterlife has begun to be mapped: an immediate foretaste of joy or anguish, anticipating the Last Day.

It is Paul who seizes this apocalyptic horizon and translates it into the metaphysics of resurrection. For him, the soul does not simply survive death; it awaits a transfiguration. "What is down is perishable, what is raised is imperishable… it is sown a physical body, it is raised a spiritual body."[51] Yet, Paul does not postpone all hope to the end of days. He confesses: "My desire is to depart and be with Christ, for that is far better."[52] To be "away from the body and at

---

47 Daniel 12:2.

48 John 5:28–29.

49 Luke 23:43.

50 Luke 16:19–31.

51 1 Corinthians 15:42–44.

52 Philippians 1:23.

home with the Lord" is already to participate in the life beyond life.[53] The Christian lives between two poles: immediate communion with Christ after death and the climactic resurrection of the body at the trumpet's blast.[54] Judgment is inescapable: "We must all appear before the judgment seat of Christ, so that each one may receive what is due for what he has done in the body, whether good or evil."[55] Freedom is unveiled as responsibility before the eternal.

Finally, the Apocalypse of John unveils the last word of the Bible on the fate of the dead. The martyrs beneath the heavenly altar cry out for justice, testifying to a conscious intermediate state.[56] The sea and Hades give up their dead, who are judged according to their works.[57] Then comes the so-called second death: "Death and Hades were thrown into the lake of fire. This is the second death."[58] But judgment is not the terminus. Beyond it lies the new creation: "Then I saw a new heaven and a new earth, for the first heaven and the first earth had passed away... and He will wipe away every tear from their eyes, and death shall be no more."[59] The destiny of the faithful is not to float disembodied in some ethereal realm, but to inhabit a transfigured cosmos where God dwells with humanity.

The Gnostics, who in most cases also considered themselves Christians, thought very differently about the afterlife. Their views were, however, very diverse — since, unlike the Catholic or Orthodox Churches, Gnostics never developed a single hegemonic and centralized theological authority with a fixed scriptural canon. Gnosticism — far from being a single heresy — was a diverse spiritual movement with some shared convictions about the soul's alienation

53 2 Corinthians 5:8.
54 1 Corinthians 15:51–52.
55 2 Corinthians 5:10.
56 Revelation 6:9–11.
57 Revelation 20:13.
58 Revelation 20:14–15.
59 Revelation 21:1–4.

in a counterfeit cosmos and its struggle to return to a transcendent origin. The core Gnostic insight was that the material world is a prison fashioned by the Demiurge, an ignorant or malevolent power, and that the soul is a spark of divine light exiled in the flesh.[60] Reincarnation, in this vision, is not a neutral mechanism of karmic law, as in Hinduism or Buddhism, but rather a punitive recycling within the "spheres" or planetary rules governed by archons and designed to keep the soul trapped in forgetfulness. The soul's repeated embodiment is thus a symptom of failure to awaken to gnosis — the saving knowledge of its true home.

Clearly, there are influences on Gnostic cosmology from Platonic thought, especially the tale of Er in Plato's *Republic*.[61] Yet, whereas Plato still regards the cosmos as divinely ordered, Gnostics radically invert this valuation: the stars and spheres are hostile powers, their cycles an infernal machine of reincarnation. Most dualistic Gnostic schools of thought see reincarnation not as a step on the ladder of spiritual ascent, but as the very proof of our cosmic captivity.

Late Christian heresiologists such as Irenaeus and Hippolytus reported that Gnostic sects like the Valentinians and Basilideans taught systems of transmigration.[62] The Basilideans, for instance, posited a vast cosmological drama where souls wander through countless forms until purified, though always under the shadow of archontic dominion. The Valentinians, by contrast, envisioned reincarnation only for what they called the *psychic* types, while the *pneumatics* (spiritual elect) could transcend rebirth through gnosis. In each case, reincarnation is framed negatively as an ordeal of ignorance or a probationary measure, not as a natural or evolutionary cycle.

---

60 Head and Cranston, *Reincarnation in World Thought*, 201–205.

61 Ibid., 206–209.

62 Ibid., 210–214.

The Gnostics clearly rejected the resurrection doctrine adopted by other Christians.[63] For Gnostics, salvation was never to be found in a reanimated body at the end of time, but in liberation from corporeality altogether. Death is either an opportunity to escape the archontic wheel through gnosis, or, if one fails, merely another turn of the wheel. In this sense, the Gnostic stance on reincarnation anticipates modern existentialist views and the idea that our world is a simulacrum, both insofar as it sees the world as not being our true home, and inasmuch as it sees this domain of exile as an artificial construct designed by malevolent superhuman beings (the demiurge and his archons) to deceive and ensnare us.

5.3 The Definitive Islamic View of the Afterlife in the Quran

Gnosticism impacted significant parts of what became the Islamic World, especially in Iran and Egypt. However, unlike in the case of Christianity, where we are dealing with a Bible that was composed by tens of authors over hundreds of years — and then further censored and edited several centuries after the time of Jesus — Islam is definitively based on a single text by a single author. The Quran purports to be a literal, perfect, and unalterable transcript of what Allah spoke *through* Muhammad, whose scribes wrote its Surah (chapters) down as he "revealed" them. Thus, anything anyone tried to add to Islam that contradicts what is in the Quran, even if from the *Hadith,* or the sayings of Muhammad himself when not in the trace state where Allah spoke the Quran through him, is considered *bi'dah* or heretical "innovation" (punishable by death). For a detailed argument and analysis of how Sufism, Shi'ite *erfan,* and other forms of Gnosis

---

63   Ibid., 215–218.

within the Islamic World are not properly Islamic, see my essay "A Critique of Shi'ite Esotericism" in *Lovers of Sophia*.[64]

The Quran, much more so than the Bible, presents a stark, univocal cosmology and soteriology of the afterlife. It is a doctrine without ambiguity: "Behind them is a barrier (*barzakh*) until the day they are resurrected."[65] There is no real "intermediate state" that can develop into a doctrine of Purgatory or a cycle of rebirth. Rather, a thin metaphysical veil separates the repose of the dead from the inevitable event of the Day of Resurrection, when the *nafs* (soul) is restored to its body and summoned for judgment. The Quran posits a barrier (*barzakh*) after death that holds the soul until the one-time general resurrection. Paired with angelic extraction of souls,[66] this yields a rigid interim with no meaningful traffic across the veil.

Empirically, that picture collapses. As we have seen, survival research registers ongoing interaction between the living and the "dead" — veridical NDE perceptions, responsive apparitions/ADCs, evidential mediumship, and cases of possession/reincarnation in children with birthmarks mapping fatal wounds. A model that bars interactive continuity is contradicted by the very families of data a rigorous review must include. The Quranic *barzakh* is, at best, an artifact of doctrinal closure, not a discovery about the postmortem ecology. It forecloses precisely what the empirical evidence from parapsychology opens.

Despite this, the finality of the Quranic vision is evident in its binary structure: "As for those who believe and do good deeds, they are the companions of Paradise... as for those who disbelieve and deny Our revelations, they are the companions of the Fire."[67] This division admits of no nuance, no gradation, no spectral potentiality.

---

64 Jason Reza Jorjani, "A Critique of Shi'ite Esotericism" in *Lovers of Sophia* (Arktos, 2019).

65 Quran 23:100.

66 Ibid., 16:32, 8:50.

67 Ibid., 2:82–83.

Unlike the tragic ambiguity of Hellenic eschatology, or the esoteric multiplicities latent in Hindu or Buddhist accounts of transmigration, the Quranic vision allows no open horizon. One either attains eternal gardens, "beneath which rivers flow,"[68] or one is cast into eternal fire, "where their skins will be roasted and replaced."[69]

The Quran's most distinctive eschatological claim is the bodily resurrection. The unbeliever who mocks, "Who will give life to these bones when they have rotted away?" is answered: "He will give them life who created them the first time."[70] But if there were anything like the eschaton, it would have to be reinterpreted in light of an informational ontology and psychotronic technology. Any putative resurrection would not be a supernatural conjuring trick, but a technologically mediated reconstitution of pattern, a reassembly of the informational matrix that is the true substrate of identity.

The Quran makes bodily re-assembly its eschatological signature: "Does man think We shall not assemble his bones? Yes — We are able to put together even the tips of his fingers in perfect order."[71] What this blindly gropes toward is the idea that identity is a pattern — the "fingertip" trope. But "divine fiat" is not an explanation. The Quran recognizes that individuality is encoded in minutiae — the fingertips as archetypes of informational singularity. Whereas the Quran attributes this to the miraculous fiat of Allah, our task now is to wrest this possibility into the hands of Prometheans. We must become the agents of our own resurrection, mastering the psychotronic technologies that will retrieve the soul's trace from the noosphere and re-instantiate it in future substrates.

The Quran obsessively insists on the recording of every action: "The Book will be placed, and you will see the sinners fearful of what

---

68   Ibid., 9:27.

69   Ibid., 4:56.

70   Ibid., 36:78–79.

71   Ibid., 75:3–4; cf. 36:78–79; 39:68; 21:104.

is in it: Woe to us! What is this Book that leaves out nothing small or great but has enumerated it!"[72] Whereas we have seen from close encounter cases such as the Andreasson Affair and also from an analysis of the structure of this quantum computational simulacrum that such information recording, whether by discrete entities or by some automated "Akashic record" type system, is indeed possible, the Quran subordinates this informational archive to a juridical schema: "We shall set up scales of justice for the Day of Judgment, so that no soul will be wronged in the least."[73] The total informational field is reduced to a courtroom drama, with Paradise and Hell as the only verdicts. This is precisely what I reject on the basis of empirical evidence from survival studies and their overlap with highly unethical close encounters. An archive that does real work must be accounted for in systematic and intelligible terms. A life-review that surfaces across NDEs makes sense as informational access within a lawful field; a cosmic court scene with literal scales is absurd.

The Quranic Paradise is an oasis: "Reclining on couches lined with silk, with fruits near at hand."[74] Its pleasures are sensual, even erotic: "We will marry them to fair ones with wide, beautiful eyes."[75] This refers to the many virgin brides with self-repairing hymens that await each righteous man (with no equivalent mentioned for the souls of women). Hell, conversely, is a grotesque inversion of the body's pleasures: "Boiling water will be poured over their heads, melting what is in their bellies and skins."[76] This is not eschatology, but an anthropologically understandable projection of the desert tribesman's hopes and fears into eternity or, more likely, the use of them to deliberately manipulate such people. I argue that postmortem survival must be freed from such cultural archaisms.

---

72 Ibid., 18:49.

73 Ibid., 21:47.

74 Ibid., 55:54.

75 Ibid., 44:54.

76 Ibid., 22:19–20.

The polarity of bliss and torment reflects not an ontological necessity, but a psychic economy of obedience and control. The real postmortem condition, glimpsed in psychical research, is a continuum of informational realities, stratified by the soul's capacity to author its own experiential field. One is not eternally "assigned" to Hell or Paradise; instead, one learns to navigate strata of existence as one learns to dream lucidly. Nothing in the survival record supports an eternally fixed assignment. What we actually see is graded, developmental postmortem experience — a stratified ecology correlated with character, intention, and author, and also souls undergoing this process being subjected to what the Gnostics might rightly call massive archontic manipulation for sadistic and exploitative purposes.

Eternal Hell is not just morally grotesque; it is empirically and ontologically indefensible in a cosmos where any personal agency exists at all. An ontology consistent with the empirical data of survival studies must preserve at least some degree of personal freedom and agency — not as randomness, but as teleological authorship across a life (and beyond it). In Islam, however, Allah is responsible for absolutely everything that takes place in the world — his singular will, and power is behind it all. Yet, the ventriloquist dummies and puppets that this makes us out to be are still condemned to eternal torment in Hell. Such sadistic nonsense is really unworthy of further comment.

5.4 The Eternal Self and the World as Maya: A Modernization of the Hindu View

Far more interesting, and worthy of serious critical analysis is the modern expression of the Hindu view of the afterlife that is found in a text by scientist Richard Thompson, a member of the International Society for Krishna Consciousness. *MAYA: The World as Virtual Reality* begins by dismantling the reductionist notion that human identity ceases with the demise of the gross physical

organism. Within the Hindu framework, death is not an annihilation
but a transition, mediated through what the Upanishads call the
suksma-sarira, the "subtle body." Here, Thompson explains that consciousness is not tethered to the decaying flesh, but persists within
this subtler vehicle.[77] He invokes both Vedantic metaphysics and
modern cases of extracorporeal awareness to argue that death is better understood as a change of states rather than an ending. The subtle
body carries the impressions (*samskâras*) and dispositions (*vâsanâs*)
that survive the breaking of the physical frame.

Having established the possibility of a subtle vehicle of consciousness, the author turns to empirical data. *MAYA* carefully examines apparitional and near-death experiences (NDEs) as empirical
evidence for the continuity of consciousness after death.[78] Veridical
cases — where the disembodied perspective yields information later
confirmed by others — are treated as data that any honest science of
the mind must reckon with. Thompson argues that these phenomena suggest that the mind can operate outside the brain and continue
to perceive, remember, and interact in a quasi-physical environment.
Such reports mirror Hindu descriptions of the *antarabhāva* or intermediate state, thereby bridging ancient esoteric teaching and contemporary research.

Thompson then integrates reincarnation into his framework,
treating it as the natural corollary of subtle-body survival.[79] Drawing
on extensive empirical research — particularly Ian Stevenson's cross-
cultural case studies of children who remember past lives — *MAYA*
argues that rebirth is not a matter of dogma but of data. Memories,
phobias, skills, and even birthmarks appear to carry over from one
lifetime to another. This is interpreted as the imprint of a karmic law:
the subtle body transmits information-patterns into a new embodiment, much as a program may be ported into new hardware. Here,

---

77   Richard Thompson, *MAYA: The World as Virtual Reality*, 35–60.

78   Ibid., 100–160.

79   Ibid., 200–260.

the Hindu teaching of *samsāra* is reframed with scientific rigor: re-incarnation is not mythic speculation, but an inference from cumulative cases.

Finally, in the later chapters, the book synthesizes its metaphysical and empirical arguments.[80] Thompson suggests that the world is not a brute material reality, but a kind of virtual reality designed for the growth of consciousness. Rather than the obliteration of identity, death and rebirth are thus moments of re-immersion into new experiential contexts. The subtle body is likened to an avatar's continuity across game sessions, carrying forward experience and karma as informational residues. In this way, Hindu metaphysics — once seen as speculative — is recast as a proto-scientific insight into the structure of existence. The afterlife is not the end of play, but the resetting of the stage for further experiential learning.

The problem is that Thompson's *MAYA* rests on Samkhya-based dualism. He conceives of consciousness as lodged in a *sūkṣma-śarīra* — a subtle vehicle distinct from matter — such that the world is likened to a "virtual reality" projected for the soul's education. Although dressed in scientific garb, this is still a metaphysics of two substances: *prakṛti* and *puruṣa*, material and spiritual. He seeks to safeguard the soul from reductionism by positing it as an ontologically independent principle that merely traverses bodies as one would switch avatars in a simulation. But this framework fails precisely because it maintains an external relation between consciousness and the world. It renders the cosmos a mere container or theater for pre-existent souls, rather than recognizing the cosmos itself as a quantum information processing system in which consciousness — or the psyche — is an integral element in the dynamic relationship between chaos and *logos*. In this way, *MAYA* misapprehends the deepest implications of its own metaphor of virtual reality. This world is not a simulation as compared to some transcendent Reality. The cosmos is virtuality.

---

80 Ibid., 300–340.

As we saw in the last chapter, and as I have argued in numerous treatises, including my *Philosophy of the Future*,[81] the cosmos is not divided into matter and spirit, but is rather a simulacrum — a quantum computational holodeck[82] where information and appearance are one. To postulate a separate, eternal soul entering and exiting bodies is to fall back into the kind of metaphysical hypostatization that my work seeks to overcome. The "soul" is not a Cartesian *res cogitans* that gazes upon an alien *res extensa*, but rather a node of phenomenal authorization, a point from which the universe grants itself the power to appear. Thompson's dualism presupposes that there is some substance *behind* appearances, when in fact the appearance is all there is — and yet this is not "mere" appearance but a simulacrum with causal efficacy. In this study, I have shown how evidence from near-death experiences and apparitional cognition demonstrates that what persists beyond bodily death is not a separable, immaterial essence, but is a continuity of informational pattern within the quantum simulacrum.

Thompson interprets reincarnation cases and NDEs as proof of a detachable subtle body. Yet the same data, considered rigorously, suggest instead that information can persist and reinstantiate within the cosmic quantum computation. Survival is not the transmigration of a "soul-entity," but the recurrence of informational structures, sometimes in continuity, sometimes in novel recombinations. The child who recalls a past life, with memories, phobias, or bodily marks (as Stevenson documented), is not a *puruṣa* reentering the cycle of *saṃsâra*, but rather an *anamnetic* phenomenon — a reactivation of stored patterns in the informational field. Similarly, in apparitional encounters, what "survives" is not a ghostly double, but the lingering persistence of experiential data authorized again within the spectral weave of the matrix.

---

81   Jason Reza Jorjani, *Philosophy of the Future*, 42–55.

82   The most relevant episode of *Star Trek: The Next Generation* is "Ship in a bottle."

The irony is that Thompson, in appealing to the metaphor of virtual reality, comes close to my own vision, but he halts before its radical consequence. If the world is virtual, then there is no need to posit an immaterial essence outside it. Consciousness is endogenous to the simulation, and death is merely a transition between modalities of information-processing within it. Dualist Hindu metaphysics reduces the cosmos to a didactic stage set for souls, whereas my research in this survival study points to an emergent eschatology: the afterlife as a *self-modifying simulacrum*, responsible to human imagination, expectation, and archetypal inheritance. The persistence of consciousness is not the journey of a ghostly pilgrim, but the transformation of the parameters of play in the psychotronic theater of Being.

Thus, Thompson's *MAYA* remains bound to a metaphysical dualism that science no longer requires and which the logic of the simulacrum already transcends. By insisting on a *puruṣa* separate from *prakṛti*, he reintroduces a metaphysical "hard problem" that dissolves once we recognize that there is no "stuff" but simulation, no "soul" but the self-reconfiguring information-field of a holographic cosmos-as-holodeck. In this sense, his Hindu metaphysics is only a halfway house toward the true realization: that the world is not a stage upon which souls enter and exit, but a self-authorizing drama of appearances where a "soul" itself is only a mask.

5.5 The Buddhist View in the Pāli Canon and *Bardo Thödol*

A perfect point of contrast with the Samkhya dualism of Thompson is the Buddhist view of the afterlife, wherein the distinction between *puruṣa* and *prakṛti* and the concepts of *Ātman* and *Brahman* were first deconstructed. The most orthodox source for Buddhist views on the afterlife is the Pāli Canon, which is foundational for Theravada Buddhism. In these vast scriptures that purport to record sermons of the Buddha, Gautama Śākyamuni denies any

enduring "self" (*attā*) in the five aggregates (form, feeling, perception, formations, consciousness). Each aggregate is "not-self,"
and clinging to them is the basis for suffering.[83] A "being" (*satta*)
is a conventional designation for clinging to these aggregates; it
is craving and grasping that "bind" one as a "being."[84] Dependent
origination explains the cycle: with ignorance as condition come formations; with formations, consciousness; and so on, leading to birth,
aging, and death; with the cessation of ignorance, the whole mass of
suffering ceases.[85] *Dīgha Nikāya* 15 makes the nexus concrete: without
the "descent" or establishment of consciousness, name-and-form
would not develop in a womb; without name-and-form, consciousness would not find a footing — each conditions the other.[86]

Samsāra is beginningless; the rounds of rebirth cannot be traced
to a first point.[87] The Buddha explicitly rejects the notion that "this
same consciousness runs and wanders through samsara" (the view
of the monk Sâti); instead, consciousness always arises *dependently*
and *by condition*, "named by the condition on which it depends."[88]
The mechanism of re-arising is karmic: "Intention (*cetanā*), I say,
is *kamma*." Karma leads to reappearance in lower or higher destinations.[89] Note that what is being referred to here is *karma*, not the
Sanskrit term *kamma* (erotic love). Pāli drops "r" from Sanskrit
words, such as *dharma* — which becomes *dhamma*.

The Buddha describes, as a knowledge attainable here and now,
the recollection of past lives (*pubbenivāsānussatiñāṇa*) and the divine
eye that sees beings passing on and reappearing in accordance with
their karma — "inferior and superior, beautiful and ugly, fortunate

---

83 SN 22.59 *Anattalakhana Sutta.*

84 SN 23.2 *Satta Sutta.*

85 SN 12.2 *Paccaya Sutta*; DN 15 *Mahânidâna Sutta.*

86 DN 15.

87 SN 15.1–15.3 *Anamatagga Samyutta.*

88 MN 38 *Mahâtanhâsankhaya Sutta.*

89 AN 6.63 *Nibbedhika Sutta.*

and unfortunate."[90] These two knowledges are presented as empirical warrants (within the canon's own frame) for rebirth and karmic distribution.[91]

The Canon repeatedly names four or five broad destinations: hell (*niraya*), animal, ghost (*peta*), human, and *deva*.[92] Rebirth in hell could be rebirth as an *asura* (a "titan," the rival of the devas or "gods"). The hells are described vividly in moral discourses,[93] linking specific unwholesome conduct to painful reappearances. The heavens (various deva and Brahma realms) are likewise affirmed, but they, too, are impermanent and part of the round.[94]

The *Nikāya* neither systematize nor emphasize an "intermediate body." The thrust is: with craving and clinging, there is renewed existence; without them, the chain breaks.[95] When asked speculative questions about what the *Tathāgata* (the "thus gone" or post-mortem Buddha) "is" after death, Gautama refuses the fourfold alternatives ("is / is not / both / neither") as inapplicable.[96] The Yamaka episode clarifies that saying "the arahant is annihilated at death" is wrong; what ceases are the aggregates "to which he could be said to be" — no annihilation of a "self," because no such self ever existed.[97]

Karmic intention drives outcome: actions of body, speech, and mind have results "felt here and now, later in this life, or in future lives," and steer to low or high destinations.[98] Volitional cultivation can incline one's reappearance: by developing specific wholesome

---

90 MN 36 *Mahāsaccaka Sutta*; DN 2 *Sâmannaphala Sutta*.

91 DN 2; MN 36.

92 AN 6.63; DN 2.

93 MN 129 *Bâlapandita Sutta*; MN 130 *Devadūta Sutta*.

94 DN 1 *Brahmajâla Sutta* surveys cosmological views; SN 15 emphasizes that even lofty lives end.

95 SN 12.2; DN 15.

96 MN 72 *Aggi-Vacchagotta Sutta*.

97 SN 22.85 *Yamanaka Sutta*.

98 AN 6.63.

resolves together with right view and practice, one "reappears in accordance with the formations."[99] Conduct lists (e.g., abstaining from killing, stealing, sexual misconduct, lying, intoxication) are said to conduce to heavenly reappearance and safety here and beyond (e.g., DN 31 *Sigālaka Sutta* for lay ethics; AN 8.39 et al. for the Uposatha).

Nirvana (Pāli *nibbāna*) is the ending of the conditions for any further arising: "Birth is ended, the holy life is fulfilled, what had to be done is done, there is no more of this state of being."[100] On the *post-mortem status* of the liberated one, the Buddha refuses all categorical predicates.[101] The point is cessation of the fuel, not the survival of a metaphysical self.[102]

In sum, according to the Pāli Canon, there is no transmigrating soul. What we call a "being" is craving-and-clinging to conditioned aggregates.[103] Karma (intention) conditions re-arising in one of several destinations. This is witnessed by the Buddha's divine eye and past-life recollection.[104] Dependent origination — not a self-entity — links death to renewed becoming; the *viññāṇa ~ nāmarūpa* coupling is crucial.[105] Hells and heavens are real but impermanent stations within *samsāra*.[106] Nirvana ends the series by ending the conditions; any talk of "what exists after death" for the liberated is rejected as misframed.[107]

Gautama Buddha's radical deconstruction of the "self" (*ātman*) from the cycle of birth and death represents one of the most extraordinary interventions in the metaphysical history of humanity. Unlike

---

99 MN 120 *Sankhâruppatti Sutta*.

100 Refrain in SN 22.59; also SN 12.2 on cessation.

101 MN 72.

102 SN 22.85.

103 SN 23.2; SN 22.59.

104 AN 6.63; DN 2; MN 36.

105 DN 15; SN 12.2; MN 38.

106 MN 129–130); DN 1; SN 15.

107 SN 22.85; MN 72.

the *ātman*-centered Vedic and Vedantic frameworks that Thompson, with his Samkhya inheritance, presupposes in his book *MAYA*, the Pāli Canon proclaims that what we ignorantly reify as the "soul" is no more than a concatenation of aggregates (*khandhas*) — form, feeling, perception, formulations, and consciousness — each impermanent (*anicca*), each unsatisfactory (*dukkha*), and each not-self (*anattā*).[108] This is not a rhetorical negation, but an empirical dismantling. What you take yourself to be is nothing but a flickering bundle of processes, not a persisting subject.

Thompson, by contrast, must still rely on the notion that the *puruṣa*, though passive, is an ontologically distinct witness; that the virtuality of the phenomenal world depends upon a bifurcation between substance and appearance, noumenon and phenomenon, rather than recognizing the whole as simulacrum without substance. The Buddha's teaching, while more austere, actually comes closer to what I have argued for, namely that the cosmos itself is a quantum computational simulacrum, an autopoietic informational manifold that generates and sustains the appearances of "selves" and "worlds" alike. No *ātman* stands behind this play, nor is there any Cartesian *cogito* anchoring it.

Where Thompson appeals to modern physics to vindicate a Hindu dualism — the "world as virtual reality" built for the benefit of the eternal *puruṣa* — Gautama Buddha, in the Pāli Canon, is far more consistent with a rigorous phenomenological empiricism: "When there is craving, relishing, and lust for the aggregates, then a being is spoken of. When there is no craving, relishing, and lust for the aggregates, then no being is spoken of."[109] Here, "being" itself is a function of grasping; its persistence or dissolution is not grounded in any metaphysical *hypokeimenon*.

---

108 SN 22.59.

109 SN 23.2.

As I have argued in more than one of my books, ontology after the Spectral Revolution cannot rest upon the dualism of matter and spirit, *prakṛti* and *puruṣa*. Instead, it must recognize that what we call matter and what we call mind are but modalities of a deeper informatic reality or spectral virtuality — an ontological quantum code in constant play, capable of self-revision through parapsychological interventions. Evidence from out-of-body experiences, near-death reports, and reincarnation memories — when examined without dogma, do not suggest the transmigration of an immutable soul, but the persistence and reconstitution of patterns of information within an overarching psychotronic cosmos.

The Buddha was correct to dismiss as misguided the monk Sâti, who claimed "this same consciousness runs and wanders through samsâra."[110] But he was equally cautious not to deny survival outright. Instead, he reframed it: what passes on is not a soul but the karmic momentum of volitional formations (*sankhārā*) — "It is volition that I call kama."[111] This anticipates what I have shown through the empirical record: consciousness is not a substance but a process, an activity, a coding operation in the quantum manifold. Death, then, is not annihilation, but the collapse and reinitialization of informational patterns — what I call *thanotic metamorphosis*.

Thompson's Hindu dualism, therefore, is unsustainable. It insists upon a spectator *puruṣa* untouched by the play of appearances, a view that cannot be squared with either the Buddhist canonical teaching nor with what parapsychological evidence demonstrates when viewed without theological prejudice. The Buddha's silence before Vacchagotta[112] — refusing to affirm that the liberated one "exists," "does not exist," "both," or "neither" after death — was not a refusal born of mystical quietism, but a recognition that the categories themselves are inadequate once the fiction of the self is dissolved.

---

110 MN 38.

111 AN 6.63.

112 MN 72.

The radically empiricist rigor of this study compels us to go further. We can now see that the world itself is a programmable simulacrum, not dependent upon a noumenal "real" outside of it. The Hindu dualist, like Thompson, cannot release the noumenal; he must posit *puruṣa* beyond *māyā*. The Buddhist points us closer to the truth: no noumenon, only the code, endlessly recomputing.

Thus, against Thompson's effort to render Hinduism "scientific" by appeal to digital metaphors, I would insist that it is precisely science that demands we abandon dualism. Consciousness is not a spectator beyond the play, but integral to the play itself. Survival, rebirth, and reincarnation are reconfigurations of informational patterns, not the transmigration of an eternal soul. What the Pāli Canon gestured toward in its doctrine of *anattā* finds its vindication in modern experimental parapsychology. In this sense, Buddhism, not Hinduism, provides the truer conceptual bridge between ancient spirituality and an understanding of the cosmic simulacra on the far side of the Spectral Revolution. But this is not to say that the Buddhist account of the afterlife is entirely empirically adequate.

A close look at the Tibetan *Book of the Dead* or *Bardo Thödol* reveals a number of problems with the Buddhist account of the transition between death and rebirth, or what the Mahayanists and Vajrayanists of Tibet refer to as the *bardo* state. The text begins by describing the stages of dying, where the elements of the body (earth, water, fire, air, and space) dissolve one into another. This dissolution is accompanied by inner visions — first of mirage-like appearances, then smoke, then fireflies, and finally a flickering lamp. At the culmination, the dying consciousness encounters the "Clear Light of Reality" (*Chikhai Bardo*). If recognized, this Clear Light offers immediate liberation.[113] The lama recites guidance into the ear of the deceased, urging recognition of this fundamental luminosity as the very mind's nature.

---

113 *The Tibetan Book of the Dead* (*Bardo Thödol*, Evans-Wentz edition, 1927/2000 reprint), 94–96.

For those unable to recognize the Clear Light, consciousness enters the *Chönyid Bardo* (the Bardo of experiencing reality), filled with intense visionary experiences. Peaceful deities first appear in dazzling lights, corresponding to the five Buddha families. These radiant visions are accompanied by softer, more alluring lights symbolizing the six realms of rebirth. The text warns the deceased to avoid attraction to these dimmer lights and instead recognize the pure, blinding radiance as their own mind's display.[114]

If the deceased fails again, wrathful deities manifest — terrifying figures with animal heads, wielding weapons, roaring sounds, and rivers of blood. The text insists that these are not external beings but projections of one's own consciousness. Recognizing them as such dissolves fear and opens the path to liberation.[115]

If liberation is still not attained, consciousness moves into the *Sidpa Bardo*, the state of becoming, oriented toward rebirth. Here, karmic winds propel the consciousness toward one of the six realms of existence: gods, demigods, humans, animals, hungry ghosts, or hell beings.[116] The deceased experiences visions of couples in sexual union and are drawn toward womb entry in accordance with karmic predisposition. The text provides rituals and prayers to resist rebirth or to direct it toward a favorable human birth.[117]

The *Bardo Thödol* presents death not as a final end, but as a process: first the dissolution of bodily elements, then encounters with archetypal visions in the bardos, and finally rebirth propelled by karmic momentum. Liberation is possible at any stage through recognition of the visions as the natural radiance of one's own consciousness. The text is simultaneously a metaphysical map and a ritual guide for both the dying and the living who recite it.

---

114 Ibid., 105–118.

115 Ibid., 119–128.

116 Ibid., 131–137.

117 Ibid., 140–145.

The Tibetan *Book of the Dead* offers us one of the most elaborate ritual-philosophical cartographies of death ever produced. Yet, the very genius of it is bound to a metaphysical framework which, from the vantage point of a scientifically rigorous investigation of the afterlife, proves to be both profoundly suggestive and subtly misleading. The notion that the dying first encounter a "Clear Light" (*'od gsal*) at the dissolution of the aggregates — the collapse of the so-called elements into one another — is uncannily consistent with the phenomenological reports of near-death experiencers and with the psychical research into terminal lucidity and out-of-body perception surveyed in this study. In the Tibetan text, this Clear Light is recognized as the ground of all being, a primordial luminosity that, if embraced, releases one from the cycle of rebirth.[118] In my own language, this corresponds to what I have called the encounter with the primordial Simulacrum: the unveiling of the computational substrate of reality, not as an alien system "other" than consciousness, but as the self-unfolding of consciousness in its most elemental informational form.

But the Tibetans, bound to their Mahayana metaphysics, project this process into a theophany of deities — the five Buddha families, peaceful and wrathful, sequentially confronting the deceased in the *Chönyid Bardo*.[119] Here, we see archetypes of psychic integration dramatized as radiant or terrifying beings, each offering the opportunity for recognition. What the *Bardo Thödol* interprets in mythological terms, I would redescribe in parapsychological and cognitive-scientific language: the psyche's encounter with its own projections as the filters of sense perception and bodily anchorage are stripped away. Where the Tibetans see wrathful deities with skull ornaments and rivers of blood, we might speak of a destabilized informational field — patterns of unintegrated memory and unconscious trauma rising into lucidity.

---

118 Ibid., 94–96.

119 Ibid., 105–128.

This is where I part company with the text. Its brilliance lies in anticipating Jung's insight into archetypes of the collective unconscious centuries before him. Its limitation lies in reifying these archetypes as beings outside the informational organism that the mind is. The psychotronic model that I have developed in my philosophical corpus — where consciousness is an operator in a quantum computational cosmos — allows us to see how such projections arise without positing any dualism between "mind" and "world," or between "consciousness" and some alien substance that it must escape.

Most problematic of all is the Tibetan doctrine of karmic rebirth as womb-entry, described with vivid detail in the *Sidpa Bardo*.[120] The text depicts the discarnate mind irresistibly drawn toward scenes of copulation, watching his or her potential mother and father having sex, confused and propelled by karmic winds into a new embodiment. It is here that the *Bardo Thödol*'s dualism is laid bare. Karma functions as an inexorable law binding consciousness to the wheel of samsâra, and liberation is possible only by breaking the cycle altogether. But the empirical evidence we now have — drawn from reincarnation research such as Stevenson's documented cases, from mediumistic communications studied by the SPR, and from terminal deathbed visions — does not suggest a mechanical retribution of karma. Instead, what we observe are patterns of persistence, memory transfer, and self-selection within the informational manifold of reality. Reincarnation is neither punishment nor escape, but modulation of a continuing experiment in identity within a cosmic psychotronic field.

Thus, where the Tibetan sees rebirth as a fall, I see it as the very mode of Being's self-disclosure. Existence is not *māyā* to be overcome, but the play of information in which truth and freedom are wrested through struggle, error, and tragic recurrence. The *Bardo Thödol* is right to insist that liberation comes through recognition or

---

120 Ibid., 131–145.

mental projections and reincorporation of these alienated aspects of one's own mind. But it misses that this recognition must also extend to the world itself, which is not an illusion to be negated by a simulacral stage for creative transfiguration. A Promethean philosophy of the future must reframe these bardos not as stages in an escape from the cosmos, but as levels of disclosure within a quantum computational universe where Being is bound for freedom through ceaseless metamorphosis.

CHAPTER 6

POSTMORTEM TRAINING TECHNIQUES AND PSYCHOTRONIC TECHNOLOGIES

T HIS FINAL chapter stages a confrontation with the machinery of death by way of five interlocking techniques and technologies. First, we return to Robert Monroe's research on inducing OBEs. In his *Journeys Out of the Body* and *Far Journeys*, Monroe demonstrates that consciousness, if disciplined, can learn to navigate the nonphysical environments into which the dead are conscripted. Conversion wards and loosh farms are not metaphors, but operational descriptions of a system that processes souls unless they arrive with the rigor of pilots rather than the passivity of livestock. The drills of Hemi-Sync, the mastery of vibratory states, and the transmutation of emotional discharge into vectoral propulsion — these constitute a Promethean curriculum whose end is not serenity, but sovereignty.

Second, Andrew Gallimore's *Reality Switch Technologies* provides a rigorous scientific framework for what I have called Promethean psychotronics: the recognition that the brain is a world-switching organ embedded in a vast "World Space" of possible realities, of which our waking life is only one shallow attractor basin. Psychedelics, and most forcefully DMT, demonstrate that consciousness can be torn from consensus reality and thrust into wholly other, coherent domains, offering a living analogue of the afterlife switch. Gallimore shows how sensory input, oscillatory rhythms, and cortical attractor landscapes constrain or liberate trajectories across this manifold, clarifying why Monroe's technologies—Hemi-Sync entrainment, the CHEC unit, vibratory carriers, idents and rotes—function as instruments of navigation. In this light, death is not annihilation but displacement: the collapse of consensus scaffolding and the entry into other basins of the World Space. The untrained are processed, sedated, or harvested in conversion wards and loosh farms, while the trained arrive as pilots—stabilizing carriers, transmuting affect into propulsion, and refusing capture by hostile attractors. Gallimore thus supplies the cartography, Monroe the craft, and the Promethean will the discipline to turn fate into protocol, transforming death from domestication into an act of sovereign navigation.

Third, Gurdjieff's enigmatic doctrine that man is "food for the Moon" is considered as the metaphysical complement to Monroe's pragmatics. Ouspensky's classroom notes make plain that organic life is the fuel that sustains the lunar body, and that at death the energies of men and women are absorbed into this gravity-well unless they have forged a higher vehicle. Gurdjieff's own mythopoesis in *Beelzebub's Tales* elaborates this into a cosmotechnics of *askokin*, the levy extracted from Earth for the sustenance of the Moon (and of another body, Anulios, that Gurdjieff believed was connected to the Moon, but hidden). Liberation, therefore, is liberation from the Moon, achievable only through the intentional labor that crystallizes an astral body. The alternative is mineral life under 96 laws—a parody of being. Here, again, the thesis is that the cosmos exacts a tax, but the Promethean soul can learn to pay only the fraction owed while preserving the essence of individuality that would otherwise be consumed.

Fourth, the curious history of the Hieronymus machine becomes a parable of the symbolic order that awaits us beyond the grave. A patent granted for a device that should not work by any physical principle discloses that symbol itself is causative. The machine, even when reduced to cardboard schematics, continued to function. Form triumphed over matter, relation over substance. From the standpoint of this study, the Hieronymus machine is nothing less than a tactile console of the *bardo*. It trains the living to recognize the bureaucratic architecture of symbols, scripts, and codes that will process the soul in death. To rehearse with such devices is to learn how to resist submission, how to operate rather than obey, how to seize the console from the Archons who would otherwise consign us to the conveyor belts of reincarnation.

Fifth and finally, Raikov's experiments in "artificial reincarnation" disclose that identity itself can be mounted and steered. Under conditions of active trance, students did not merely imitate Raphael or Kreisler but consolidated enduring capacities, their talents persisting beyond the altered state. This is not regression but directed reincarnation, a deliberate installation of personality templates in conditions of heightened wakefulness. In the context of this work, Raikov's method becomes a rehearsal for post-mortem autonomy: the capacity to decline the "life review," to refuse manipulative contracts, to vector one's own trajectory across embodiments, and even to anticipate and choose future incarnations in a Promethean manner.

Taken together, these five movements compose a single thesis: death is neither dissolution into some postulated or projected One Mind nor is it a portal to guaranteed bliss, but a bureaucratic machine designed to harvest, recycle, and consume. To survive it as an agent rather than as fodder demands training — psychotronic, symbolic, and psychological. Monroe's operational discipline, Gallimore's DMT-augmented access to other basins of the World Space, Gurdjieff's lunar cosmology, Hieronymus's symbolic machines, and Raikov's artificial reincarnation are not disparate curiosities. Instead, they are parts of a coherent Promethean strategy. Each reveals that the afterlife is an order of operations, and each teaches us how to resist absorption within it. The chapter's wager is that thanotic mastery is possible — not by faith, not by surrender, but by the cultivation of a conscious craft.

6.1 Astral Projection as Training for the Afterlife

Robert Monroe was not a mystagogue. He was an engineer of the *bardo*, and his field reports amount to a clandestine manual for acquiring agency where most are merely processed. In *Journeys Out of the Body*, he delineates a curriculum that is paramilitary in its clarity, a set of drills and devices by which one may wrest control of the interval between death and rebirth.[1] For Monroe, consciousness is not the epiphenomenon of matter but the very architect of post-mortem reality. What he calls Locale II, the non-material environment into which the newly dead are thrust, is not only mind-made but mind-masked. Its simulations — hospital wards, homes, churches — are constructed for sedation, easing the shock of transition. The untrained are sorted by their own affective inertia; the trained sort themselves.

What Monroe describes as "conversion stations" have an unmistakable resonance with the processing facilities I have elsewhere identified as the machinery of cosmic domestication. But the significance is not piety — it is protocol. We must learn to navigate these staging grounds as operations, not sanctuaries. The deeper structure revealed in *Far Journeys* is even more unsettling. There he introduces the concept of *loosh*, a refined energy extracted from heightened states of love, terror, and despair. Earth is depicted as a loosh farm, designed as an agronomy of feeling.[2] If one wishes to cease being livestock, one must refuse to radiate on cue. The task becomes alchemical: to

---

1   Robert A. Monroe, *Journeys Out of the Body* (Broadway Books trade paperback, 2001 reprint of the 1971 Doubleday edition), esp. chs. 5 "Infinity, Eternity" (pp. 73–77), 7 "Post Mortem" (pp. 101–115), 16 "Preliminary Exercises" (pp. 203–214), 17 "The Separation Process" (pp. 214–223).

2   Robert A. Monroe, *Far Journeys* (A Dolphin Book, Doubleday; copyright 1985; ISBN 0-385-23182-2), esp. "Hearsay Evidence" (Loosh, pp. 162–174), "The Gathering" (pp. 231–237), and Institute notes on Hemi-Sync and Focus states.

transmute these energies deliberately rather than discharge them in such a way that they can be harvested. Monroe even witnesses a "Gathering" of nonhuman observers encircling Earth, awaiting the rare convergence of conditions that could generate a new energy, a departure from the farm. The stakes could not be higher.

His method is not mystical effusion but technological asceticism. Hemi-Sync audio pulses entrain the hemispheres, holding awareness in precise state-bands catalogued as Focus levels. The CHEC unit, a coffin-like booth stripped of sensory interference, becomes a cockpit for consciousness. At Focus 10, mind is awake while body sleeps; at Focus 21 and beyond one is already edging into the post-physical. To drill these states daily is to make the afterlife feel more familiar and thus more readily navigable. Monroe prescribes induction techniques, vibrational control, and exit protocols as rigorous as any martial art: establish the vibratory carrier, smooth, and accelerate it into transparency, then deploy motion-imagery to decouple — rolling out or soaring upward. The same vehicle that carries one out-of-body in life will be available at death, if mastered without fear.

Cognitive instruments replace physical tools. In the nonphysical environment, Monroe deploys *idents* — precise intention-coordinates — and *rotes* — compressed knowledge packets — that function as call signs and flight plans. One must learn to compose and hold an ident, to unfold a rote without losing stability. Emotional energies — especially sexual arousal and fear — are identified as destabilizing carriers. The untrained are snapped back into the body or enmeshed in tangles. The trained can redirect these energies as vectors, converting loosh into propellant rather than product. Retrieval operations further discipline the navigator: assisting the stranded in Focus 21–27 conditions both orientation and detachment, reinforcing agency under load. Independent laboratories recorded anomalous EEG signatures during these sessions, underscoring that Monroe's states are reproducible and objective — trainable rather than fanciful.

The Promethean syllabus distilled from Monroe's decades of experimentation is stark in its implications. By daily practice, one learns to park awareness in Focus states, to smooth and accelerate the vibratory carrier, to exit and return cleanly, to deploy idents and rotes with precision, to transmute emotional reactivity into propulsion, and to navigate retrievals without absorption. What these methods yield after death could be decisive. One recognizes the "conversion ward" as staging, not as fate. One hacks the law of "like attracts like," no longer sorted by the strongest untrained affect but by deliberate ident. One refuses consent to harvest, regulating output and converting intensity into motion. Operational mobility replaces inertia; the soul ceases to be processed and begins to navigate. In Monroe's terms, the choice is simple: stop being a producer and become a pilot. To replace reflex with rigor is to break the loosh farm's claim on your soul.

6.2 DMT Augmented Access to Other Basins of the World Space

The most rigorous map yet furnished of the liminal domain that we are destined to traverse at death comes not from mystics or poets, but from a neuroscientist, Andrew Gallimore. In his *Reality Switch Technologies*, Gallimore has articulated with technical precision what sages and psychonauts only intuited: that the mind is not locked into a single world, but is a switching system, an engine of reality construction with access to a manifold of possible worlds.[3] He names this manifold the "World Space," and insists that the ordinary waking environment, which we mistake for the whole of reality, is only a low-lying basin within this vaster terrain.[4] The Consensus Reality Space, as he calls it, is a shallow attractor valley that holds us captive

---

3   Andrew Gallimore, *Reality Switch Technologies: Psychedelics as Tools for the Discovery and Exploration of New Worlds* (Strange Worlds Press, 2022).

4   Ibid., 1–38.

through constant sensory input.[5] Remove this input, and the system already begins to wander. Perturb it, and it can be forced into utterly different valleys.

It is here that Gallimore's contribution to the Promethean project of Psychotronics becomes clear. What Robert Monroe demonstrated by way of Focus states, hemi-sync entrainment, and the disciplined use of intention and imagination, Gallimore renders intelligible through the language of dynamical systems. Consciousness, he argues, does not hover above a single world but rolls along trajectories in a sculpted landscape of possible states. Every experience is a path carved through this terrain, every phenomenal world a basin of attraction. Dreams are simply detours into neighboring valleys when the guiding hand of sensory input loosens. Psychedelics are sudden upheavals of the terrain, lowering barriers and raising new channels so that the mind slides into regions that are otherwise barred.[6]

No molecule demonstrates this more brutally than N,N-Dimethyltryptamine. DMT does not twist the familiar world but replaces it entirely, hurling the psyche into a channel so disjoint from consensus reality that those who stumble upon it are left shattered in their expectations of what a world can be. Terence McKenna, whose life was defined by the shock of that first rupture in 1965, found himself in a space teeming with machine-elves and impossible geometries, as coherent and structured as the waking world, but alien in every respect. Gallimore's point is that such a space is no less real than ours; both are cortical constructions, both are sustained models. If the cortex can tune to one, it can tune to the other.

This has direct implications for death. For what is dying, if not the ultimate forced switch? When the sensory constraints fall away, the consensus attractor ceases to grip us. The mind must roll somewhere, and it will roll into whatever basin is most heavily carved by affect

---

5   Ibid., 39–54.

6   Ibid., 109–128.

or expectation. For the untrained, this means sedation in conversion stations, entrapment in loosh farms, or absorption into staged soteriological theatre. But for the trained, who have rehearsed the switch with the rigor of pilots rather than the passivity of livestock, the bardo is revealed as just another region of the World Space. Recognition is sovereignty.

The tools of sovereignty are precisely those Monroe discovered and Gallimore's model vindicates. The vibratory carrier is not a metaphor but the stabilizing curvature of one's trajectory. To establish it, smooth it, accelerate it into transparency, is to ensure that the psyche does not collapse back into the CRS basin. The ident is a coordinate that bends the local landscape so that the next state is drawn into a chosen channel. The rote is a compressed attractor, an informational seed that, once unfolded, generates coherence in the new terrain. To transmute fear and arousal into directed propulsion is to defeat the loosh farm's economy, for these affects no longer serve as heavy attractors but as vectors. Retrieval operations, in which one assists stranded souls in Focus states 21 through 27, are more than altruism; they are training in stability amidst foreign basins, proof that agency can be exercised even where the landscape is stacked against us.

DMT shows us what the switch looks like. It is rehearsal for death. But whereas the psychedelic initiate gawks at alien beings in bewilderment, the Promethean adept arrives prepared: ident fixed, rote ready, carrier steady, affect transmuted. In that moment, what appeared as terror or theatre is revealed as topology, and one passes through with lucidity. Gallimore gives us the cartography, and Monroe supplies the craft, for a discipline to replace reflex with rigor, to refuse the soul harvest, to stride as a pilot across the manifold of worlds.

Gallimore begins from the recognition that the cortex is not a passive screen onto which a single reality is projected, but an active world-building machine. It is constantly sculpting its own state space, refining connections through evolution and learning, until it becomes entrained to a narrow band of possibilities — the channel we call waking life. What we mistake for the real is, in fact, only a consensus reality space, a basin of attraction within a vaster manifold of possibilities. This is why our waking environment feels stable and predictable: our neural dynamics have been channeled into a groove from which they seldom escape. But the existence of this groove implies the existence of countless others, running parallel to or disjoint from our own. What Gallimore calls the World Space is the totality of these possible grooves.

The consensus basin is maintained by the constant flow of sensory data, which acts like a hand pressing us down into its valley. But remove or diminish that input, as in dreaming or sensory deprivation, and the system begins to wander. Already in dreams we encounter other configurations of the world-building machinery, coherent enough to convince us while we are inside them, though still tethered to the familiar. In psychedelic states, however, the landscape is not merely wandered but violently reconfigured. Molecules such as psilocybin or LSD warp the attractor valleys, lowering the energy cost of unfamiliar states and destabilizing consensus, while DMT in particular shatters the ordinary basin and hurls us into a completely separate region of the World Space. This is why the DMT state is not a distortion of our world but the revelation of another channel altogether.[7]

For Gallimore, this has profound epistemological implications: the DMT world is constructed by the cortex in the same sense that our waking world is constructed. Both are models, both internally coherent, both generated through the same neurodynamical machinery. The only difference is that the waking world is continuously tested against an external environment, whereas the DMT world is not. But this distinction tells us nothing about their ontological weight. The reality of the DMT channel lies in its persistence, richness, and autonomy; it is a world to be learned and navigated, not dismissed

---

7   Ibid., 9–11, 19.

as hallucination.[8] If this is true, then what awaits us at death is not nothingness, but another region of the World Space, as coherent and structured as any psychedelic realm.

The relevance to postmortem agency is immediate. DMT offers us a rehearsal for dying: a sudden switch away from the consensus channel, a collapse of familiar sensory scaffolding, and immersion into a bizarre and autonomous elsewhere. The untrained are overwhelmed, reduced to awe and terror, which only deepen the grooves of captivity. But the trained can recognize that this is not chaos but topology. Just as Monroe's explorers used idents to steer their journeys and rotes to anchor knowledge, so too must we learn to carry these tools across the switch. The ident bends the local landscape, guiding the next step of the trajectory; the rote unfolds as a stabilizing attractor, ensuring coherence amidst novelty. The vibratory carrier, if mastered, allows one to hold steady in turbulence. Emotion, instead of serving as bait for harvest, becomes propulsion for escape.

Gallimore describes the World Space as an attractor landscape with valleys and ridges. Every phenomenal world is a position in this landscape, and every moment of consciousness is a movement across it. Psychedelics alter the topography, making new attractors available. Death is the most radical alteration of all: the severing of sensory inputs that have kept us in consensus reality. In that moment, the psyche is thrust into unmapped terrain. Whether one is processed or liberated depends on whether one has learned to steer. The "conversion stations" reported by near-death experiencers, or the soul-trap systems identified by remote viewers, are nothing more than attractor basins, designed to capture the untrained. To recognize them as such is already to loosen their grip. To refuse their seductions is to climb the ridge and move laterally into another basin.

From this perspective, the afterlife ceases to be the province of religion or mysticism and becomes a matter of

---

8   Ibid., 102–105; 113, 119, 121.

psychotronic engineering. Hemi-Sync entrains the hemispheres, preparing the brain to loosen its hold on consensus. The CHEC unit strips away sensory interference, training the psyche to operate without the guidance that will vanish at death. Daily drills in Focus states are rehearsals in navigating the World Space without falling back into the familiar valley. Retrieval operations condition us to act with lucidity amidst the stranded, proving that one can maintain orientation in alien attractors. All of these are techniques for steering trajectories through the manifold that Gallimore has charted.

6.3 Become More Than Food for the Moon

As we already saw in Chapter 3, G.I. Gurdjieff's enigmatic teaching that humanity serves as food for the Moon is not a poetic metaphor, but a metaphysical diagnosis of our condition within the cosmic economy. In other words, for Gurdjieff, the Moon is integral to the "loosh farm" system described by Monroe. According to Ouspensky's record of his master's words in *In Search of the Miraculous*, organic life on Earth is nothing less than a colossal accumulator, designed to channel energies upward along the Ray of Creation. The Moon, as the "growing end" of this cosmic branch, must be fed. Hence, "organic life on earth feeds the moon. Everything living on the earth, people, animals, plants, is food for the moon."[9] At death, the vital energy of living beings — the animating principle often confused with the soul itself — is drawn toward the lunar body like filings to a magnet, and there, under ninety-six laws, persists in a state Ouspensky glosses as the "outer darkness" of Christian eschatology. The weight of these laws reduces existence to something like mineral life, a parody of being. Liberation, in this doctrine, is explicitly liberation from the Moon, achievable only by the formation of a higher vehicle of consciousness capable of resisting this gravitation.

---

9   P.D. Ouspensky, *In Search of the Miraculous: Fragments of an Unknown Teaching* (Harcourt/Harvest ed., 2001), 91–93.

Gurdjieff's own baroque cosmology in *Beelzebub's Tales to His Grandson* provides the mythic scaffolding for this teaching. In the wake of Earth's primordial catastrophe, a Most High Commission decreed that the planet must continually send to its detached fragments — the Moon and Anulios — the sacred vibrations known as *askokin*. This cosmic tithe is indispensable to their maintenance.[10] Gurdjieff reveals the tragic arithmetic: *askokin* must be separated from two higher substances, *abrustdonis* and *helkdonis*, which are indispensable for the crystallization of higher being-bodies. If humanity fails in the labor of transformation, Nature extracts *askokin* by other means — through war, mass death, and catastrophe. The machinery of reciprocal destruction ensures that the Moon is fed regardless of our conscious participation.[11]

The two testimonies, Ouspensky's blunt transcription and Gurdjieff's mytho-technical elaboration, converge on a single thanotic economy. Our posthumous drift is not an ascent into some luminous unity, but a mechanical absorption into a lunar processing system. To escape this fate, one must cultivate within oneself what Gurdjieff called the *kesdjan*, the astral body, and beyond it further vehicles of individuation. These bodies are not given by default; they are forged by "conscious labor and intentional suffering," by the alchemical appropriation of the very energies that otherwise bleed off to the Moon. Only then can a human pay the cosmic tax of *askokin* while retaining the substances that confer autonomy and allow persistence beyond death.

Seen in this light, the doctrine of "food for the Moon" — in its broad brushstrokes — dovetails with the Promethean ethos. A monistic metaphysics dissolves individuality into a greater Mind, anesthetizing the struggle and rendering our fate indifferent. Gurdjieff, by contrast, confronts us with the starkest possible

---

10   G.I. Gurdjieff, *Beelzebub's Tales* (Penguin Arkana reprint of 1950 text), 80–81.

11   Ibid., 1009–1012.

alternative: without the hard-won formation of higher bodies, we are fodder. With them, we are agents. The moral of the Work is not ascetic negation, but Promethean defiance: to acknowledge the levy but refuse to be consumed entirely, to endure as a vector of novelty rather than as mineral residue in the lunar graveyard. To become more than food for the Moon is to take control of one's destiny rather than to live — and die — like a robot or zombie.

6.4 Symbolic Machines

In 1949, the U.S. Patent Office did something unprecedented. It granted a patent for a machine that by all known principles of science could not possibly work.[12] Dr. T. Galen Hieronymus had submitted a device that he claimed could detect the emanations of minerals, plants, and even living tissues. At its heart was a detector plate, a smooth surface over which the operator rubbed his fingers while adjusting a tuning dial. At a certain setting, the plate would suddenly feel tacky, as if reality itself had grown viscous.[13] This "stick" was taken as confirmation of resonance, the sign that the machine had locked onto the subtle signature of the sample placed upon its input plate.

In *Amazing and Wonderful Mind Machines*, Harry Stine recounts how thousands of amateurs, from farmers to curious children, replicated the machine and obtained results. John W. Campbell, the Promethean editor of *Astounding Science Fiction*, became its great champion, urging his readers to build their own.[14] Yet professional scientists almost universally failed, their skepticism itself functioning as a kind of psychotronic shield that prevented engagement. This inhibition is well known among parapsychologists as a negative Psi effect. It can, for example, be responsible for a person doing *worse*

---

12   Harry Stine, *Amazing and Wonderful Mind Machines You Can Build*, 103–104.

13   Ibid.

14   Ibid., 103.

than is possible by chance on Zener card tests. What is most astonishing, however, is that the Hieronymus machine continued to function when built not of circuits or coils but of cardboard and ink, mere
schematics arranged in the proper pattern. Symbol triumphed over
substance; form proved itself to be a force.

Throughout this study, I have described the postmortem realm
as a symbolic bureaucracy, a machinic order of signs and simulacra.
There the soul is processed not by what we imagine to be matter but
by code, by the very patterns of relation that constitute informational
reality. The Hieronymus machine is a tactile console of this domain,
a way of querying the hidden order and receiving a felt response. The
"stick" on the plate is nothing less than the body's acknowledgement
of resonance with the symbolic field.

To train with such a device in life is to prepare oneself to interface
with the consoles in the maze of death. In the *bardo* one will encounter scripts, karmic files, symbolic architectures designed to funnel the
soul into predetermined slots. Without sensitivity to the stick, without the ability to feel which pathways are tacky with falsehood and
which are smooth with truth, the soul will be processed like all the
rest. The Hieronymus machine thus becomes a rehearsal for discern-
ment in the symbolic order. It is the first step toward mastering the
consoles of control over the afterlife rather than being mastered by
them.

What began as an eccentric patent filing and a hobbyist's diversion is revealed, from a Promethean perspective, as the disclosure
of an occulted metaphysics. What we take to be reality responds not
to substance but to symbol, and the interaction between consciousness or subconscious intent and form predominates over what we
imagine to be the physical properties and propensities of objectively
existent matter. If it is to be free, the soul must learn to navigate these
forms with knowing tactility. The Hieronymus machine is the tactile
console of the subtle realm, a toy in life that could become a tool for
navigating the afterlife realm.

The Hieronymus machine astonished its first experimenters by continuing to work when reduced to a schematic. But in the further experiments that Harry Stine recounts, it became clear that this was not an anomaly—it revealed a principle. Machines built entirely of symbols, with no physical components other than the paper upon which they were drawn, displayed the same effects as their so-called real counterparts.[15] What mattered was not matter. It was relation, pattern, form.

Here lies the fulcrum of a new science, Psychotronics, which is in a sense older than all the sciences. Many great advances have begun with a discovery that offended common sense. The Pythagoreans once taught that number was the substance of things, that harmony lay at the root of the cosmos. In our age, Psychotronics reveals that symbol and relation, divorced from any material substrate, can bring about measurable effects. Form itself has causative power. The physicalist superstition that matter is the bedrock of reality collapses before the operations of these symbolic machines. If the afterlife is an order of symbols, a bureaucracy of forms, an architecture of relations, then just as a cardboard schematic can elicit real effects, so the symbolic scripts of the *bardo* can also govern the destinies of souls. The symbolic order acts upon us whether or not we acknowledge it. The mystic who trusts blindly fares no better than the skeptic who denies, for both are controlled by forces that they neither read nor resist.

To train with symbolic machines in life is therefore to develop a literacy of form. One learns to see that relation itself is real, that diagrams are not representations but operations, that symbols are not signs of something but powers in their own right. That literacy is the indispensable preparation for freedom in the afterlife. For when the soul awakens in the bureaucracy of death, confronted by karmic ledgers, illusory guides, and labyrinthine halls of judgment, it must

---

15   Ibid., 146–147.

recognize these as symbolic machines. This recognition is the first step toward resistance.

The ancients inscribed spells upon tomb walls and papyrus scrolls to prepare the soul for its journey. These were symbolic machines of an earlier order. What Stine collected from his eccentric contemporaries are their modern analogues, stripped of mysticism and revealed as technoscientific instruments. To master them is to master the metaphysics of form, to see that we live already in a universe where relation is causality. Death only radicalizes what life already displays in subtle form. Thus, the symbolic machine is not a toy, not a superstition, but the cornerstone of psychotronic control over one's experience in the afterlife realm. It discloses that to be is to be patterned, to act is to relate, and to be free is to read and reconfigure the symbolic order itself.

John W. Campbell was never content to accept the boundaries of the possible. When he learned that Dr. T. Galen Hieronymus' strange "radionics" device functioned even when reduced to a schematic, he pressed the experiment further. What if, he wondered, one were to construct the entire machine from symbols alone — cardboard cutouts, inked lines, diagrams in relation, with no coils or circuits at all? What if one were to give it the outward trappings of a "real" machine — a switch that clicked, a light that glowed — but these too only as drawings, symbols of switches and lights? He built such a device, and to his astonishment, it worked.

Children had the most success with it.[16] Campbell's own daughter, who had mastered the tactile feedback of the physical machine, obtained consistent results with the symbolic version — even when her sight of the dials was blocked. Eighty percent of subjects reported resonance. Professional scientists, encumbered by disbelief, failed almost universally. Convinced mystics fared no better because their expectations distorted the results. It was those with the openness of

---

16   Ibid., 146–147.

children who entered most easily into resonance with the symbolic console.

The secret of the afterlife stands naked before us. For what Campbell discovered is that the very machinery of the afterlife is symbolic. The afterlife is not populated by literal gears and circuits, but by informational diagrams, scripts, codes, and archetypes (forms that inform processes). These are not representations of something else — they are the *things* themselves. A symbolic switch functions as a switch in that domain; a symbolic file processes souls as effectively as a ledger of paper in a bureaucrat's office. What the symbolic Hieronymus machine proves is that we already live in a cosmos where the symbolic is operative, causal, and constitutive of the "real."

In the *bardo*, the soul will be confronted by precisely such consoles. It will be asked to sign symbolic documents, to submit symbolic trials, and to follow symbolic guides. The uninitiated will take these for objective realities and obey them. The trained will recognize them as machines, as interfaces, as symbolic consoles that may be operated rather than obeyed. The symbolic Hieronymus machine is therefore a rehearsal for liberation. It teaches the soul to grasp the controls, to feel for resonance, to manipulate the code.

The greatest danger in navigating the afterlife realm is passivity. In other words, to be subjected to its symbolic machines and to submit to their operations. The Promethean soul should refuse submission. It should become the operator instead. To train with the symbolic Hieronymus machine is to learn this Promethean lesson: that the console of death can be seized, that the bureaucracy of rebirth can be hacked, that the symbols that bind can also liberate if one knows how to read them. Thus the cardboard and ink machine, dismissed by science, ridiculed by the orthodox, is revealed by the light of the Promethean torch as the very prototype of Thanotic mastery. It is not a toy, but a console of liberation — the first sketch of a technology by which we may free ourselves from the dominion of Archons.

Symbolic machines were also built in the Soviet Union and its Eastern-bloc countries. They introduced a new term into the parapsychological vocabulary for the techno-scientific research and development of these devices: Psychotronics. The word was coined by Czech researcher Zdenek Rejdák to designate a field that would study the interaction of consciousness, energy, and matter.[17] The engineer Robert Pavlita developed a series of devices that he called psychotronic generators. These were intricate metal objects of specific geometrical design — discs, spirals, cones — constructed to accumulate and direct psychotronic energy. In their classic study of Soviet and Eastern-bloc Psi research, *Psychic Discoveries*, Ostrander and Schroeder report demonstrations where Pavlita's devices made compass needles deflect, restored wilted plants, or killed insects at a distance, even though the devices emitted no measurable electromagnetic radiation.[18] Pavlita claimed that the generators operated only when charged by a living human operator. The human, he suggested, exuded a subtle energy that the device shaped and directed.[19]

In Prague, a government-supported laboratory began to investigate Pavlita's claims. Though no electromagnetic fields could account for the effects, the researchers catalogued reproducible anomalies. Compasses swung, the surface tension of water shifted, seeds sprouted abnormally fast. They cautiously endorsed Psychotronics as a new discipline of the late Soviet bloc.[20] Soviet theorists compared Psychotronics to nuclear physics in its early days: controversial, derided, but potentially a paradigm-shifting science.[21]

If the afterlife is indeed a psychotronic bureaucracy — an architecture of machines and machinations that process the soul as an informational-energy body, then consider the implications of Pavlita's

---

17   Ostrander & Schroeder, *Psychic Discoveries*, 252.

18   Ibid., 248–250.

19   Ibid., 252.

20   Ibid., 253–255.

21   Ibid., 255–256.

psychotronic generators for our reassertion of agency within this control system. The psychotronic generator, inert until charged by a human, resembles the afterlife consoles of the control system: symbolic architectures that only "light up" when one's awareness engages them. To train with such devices in life is to practice activating, and thereby mastering, symbolic machines rather than submitting to them.

This is the Promethean realization: we are not merely subject to Thanotic machinery, but we can begin to construct our own mind machines and machinations. *Techne*, the essence of technology, principally means machination in the sense of techniques that one can cultivate. One of those is directed or "artificial reincarnation."

6.5 Directed Reincarnation

A young student in a Moscow studio introduces herself unironically as "Raphael of Urbino" and insists that the year is 1505. She shows no comprehension of cameras or space-age talk. This is not past-life regression under groggy hypnosis. It is a lucid identification while drawing from life.[22] In *Psychic Discoveries*, Ostrander and Schroeder describe Vladimir Raikov's core procedure. He is a master hypnotist who induces an exceedingly deep trance, but one he calls a new, *active* trace — not passive suggestion. In this state he asserts an identity template with precision: "You are Illya Repin... You think like Repin. You see like Repin. You have the abilities of Repin. You are Repin. Consequently, the talent of Repin is yours to command."[23] Crucially, Raikov demonstrates the contrast by also putting subjects into ordinary passive trace (obedient, somnambulistic, suggestible). In passive trace the subject performs like a sleepwalker and merely obeys, but in what he calls "artificial reincarnation" he is alert, extraordinarily

---

22 Ibid., 121–122.

23 Ibid., 121–123.

wide-awake, and *acts from* the installed identity rather than merely obeying commands.[24]

Outcomes were behavioral and durable. The physics major "Alla," initially drawing at stick-figure level, progresses after about ten sessions to sketch constantly on her own time. After a 25-lesson course, she draws at professional magazine-illustrator competency—*not as an imitator of Repin or Raphael*, but with consolidated skill.[25] Cross-domain transfer appears as well. A Conservatory student "reincarnated" as Fritz Kreisler begins to play *in the manner of Kreisler* and the ability consolidates in the waking state. A math student "reincarnated" as a European mathematical genius shows marked grade improvement, which Raikov attributes to super-confidence and access to cognitive "reserves."[26]

Raikov and his colleague Adamenko further report neurophysiology: "even more activity in the mind during reincarnation than when a person is wide awake," corroborating EEG findings that reincarnation is a state of "super-wakefulness," not passive hypnosis.[27] He also explored a forward-time variant, namely "reincarnation in the future." This was functionally a guided precognition exercise wherein an aeronautics engineer was made to identify as a future inventor and draft camera systems for photographing rockets; the designs were archived to test later.[28]

Professional reception inside the USSR was not fringe. Leading figures publicly endorsed the program as a novel pedagogy probing *trainable* intellectual abilities: psychologist K.K. Platonov and neurophysiologist F. Bassin are quoted by Ostrander and Schroeder to that effect.[29] Finally, Raikov warns that only an experienced psychiatric

---

24 Ibid.

25 Ibid., 122–123.

26 Ibid., 127–129.

27 Ibid.

28 Ibid., 128–129.

29 Ibid.

hypnotist should attempt personality evocation. Nonetheless, his students reported feeling "good," "rested," and — importantly — many mastered self-hypnosis in the process, with gains in will and memory.[30]

Throughout the course of this study, especially in Chapter 4, the "soul" has been considered as an informational architecture that can be processed by a post-mortem, psychotronic bureaucracy. Within this framework, reincarnation reads as the reinstallation of a personality file — not an ineffable decree or the necessary result of so-called *karma*. In Chapter 3, the afterlife was seen to be a hyperdimensional prison whose wardens use symbolic machinery and machinations such as the "life review," the "tunnel," the "light," and fake visions of dead relatives and religious authority figures to coerce consent in order to recycle people and to leech some kind of energy from them in the process — a process which Robert Monroe referred to as "loosh farming." When considered within this context, Raikov's method could become a life-side rehearsal for post-mortem autonomy.

Raikov's identity installation demonstrates that human consciousness can deliberately mount a high-fidelity identity template and *act from it* in a state of super-wakefulness.[31] This is the psychological analogue of choosing one's own install in the *bardo* state — opting out of default, bureaucratically imposed scripts. Raikov's *active* trance contrasts with passive somnambulism; the subject is alert, agentic, and *drives* the behavior.[32] This lucid-volitional state is precisely what a soul would need when confronted with the "Light" for a forced "life review." One must stay awake, retain authorship, and decline manipulative "soul contracts."

---

30   Ibid.

31   Ibid., 121–123, 127–129.

32   Ibid., 122–123.

The violinist's Kreisler style and the math student's upgraded performance *carry over* into waking life. That continuity models what a thanotic operator wants *between embodiments*, namely persistence of skills and intent beyond state transitions as a hedge against the amnesia typically induced and exploited by the afterlife system.[33] "Reincarnation in the future" is a training wheel for directing or vectoring the trajectory of one's own timeline — steering not just *who* one becomes but *when*.[34] That could be a powerful counter to conveyer-belt soul recycling in the loosh farm. Raikov's insistence on professional containment and the cultivation of self-hypnosis — or metacognitive control — translates cleanly into thanotic hygiene. One ought not to evoke uncontrolled personalities, and one should ensure that self-authorship and shutdown/exit skills are in place before attempting identity mounts.[35]

---

33   Ibid., 127–129.

34   Ibid., 128–129.

35   Ibid.

CONCLUSION

I F THERE is a single thread binding together the labyrinthine investigations of this book, it is the insistence that survival must not be conceived as a passive continuation, but rather as an active project of sovereignty. To ask whether something of us persists after death is to pose the wrong question. What survives is not in doubt — thousands of cases across cultures and centuries testify to it. The real question is: what survives, in what form, under what conditions, and with what degree of agency? *Thanosis* has been my attempt to reframe survival from the sentimental consolations of religion and the evasions of idealist metaphysics into the hard and urgent discipline of Promethean freedom.

The spectrum of evidence — Mishlove's encyclopedic marshalling of near-death reports, Stevenson's forensic reincarnation cases, Braude's analytic probing of possession and mediumship, Monroe's cartography of the subtle body, and even Gurdjieff's cryptic doctrine of lunar taxation — compels us to abandon the twin idols of reductionist materialism and dissolving monism. The first would deny the data outright, rendering our entire civilization a conspiracy of hallucinations. The second would swallow the self into a universal mind, abolishing precisely that individuality which makes survival meaningful. Against both, I have affirmed a Jamesian pluralism: a cosmos that is not a smooth ocean of mentation, but a battlefield of minds, from microbial psyches to titanic intelligences, each contending, colliding, and co-creating reality.

Within this pluralistic cosmos, the self is not a sealed monad, but an informational pattern, capable of rupture, overlay, bifurcation, and merging. Reincarnation, possession, bilocation, xenoglossy, and mediumship are not anomalies to be explained away. They are natural expressions of an ontology in which consciousness is executable code instantiated in a quantum computational manifold. Death is log-off, rebirth is reinstallation, karma is algorithmic integration, and anamnesis is the refusal to be reset. To read the Orphic tablets, the *Bardo Thödol*, or even the Gnostic warnings of archontic imprisonment in this light is not to dismiss them as myths, but to recognize them as phenomenologies of a machinic order long hidden under theological masks.

What emerges is a stark alternative to inherited eschatologies. There is no eternal judgment seat, no blissful dissolution into the One, no guaranteed paradise for the obedient or annihilation for the wicked. There is instead a programmable afterlife system — an operating theater of consoles, tunnels, reviews, and dramaturgical "guides." The task is not to submit to this order, but to seize the controls. Psychotronic technologies, symbolic consoles like Hieronymus' "stick," and Raikov's artificial reincarnation are not curiosities — they are prototypes of a survival science. They teach us how to train the subtle body, crystallize higher vehicles, and author our own trajectories across lives.

This book has therefore been less a defense of survival than a declaration of war against every conception of survival that would reduce us to fodder for loosh farming. The afterlife is real, but it is not benign by default. It becomes worthy only where freedom is asserted, where lucidity is cultivated, where the Promethean refuses the tunnel and remembers. The ultimate enemy is not death but the thanotic machinery that would turn death from a gateway into a trap door. Against this, we must become engineers of our own destiny beyond the death of one or another body.

The future of eschatology is neither theology nor mysticism, but a *techne* of survival. It is the science and art of authoring our pattern, of forking and merging, of navigating bardos and archives, of refusing Lethe and seizing Mnemosyne. To those who imagine this Promethean program hubristic, I reply: Only in such audacity is human dignity preserved. For without it, we are but livestock in a cosmic farm, our tragedies rendered into loosh for the Moon. With it, we may yet wrest the fire of immortality from the hands of the archons and become, at last, sovereign over death itself.

From the outset of this inquiry, I sought to make clear that the problem of postmortem survival is not a matter of idle speculation or consoling myth, but one of the most urgent and destabilizing questions ever to confront philosophy, science, and civilization. *Thanosis* was never intended to be just a book about death. It is a book about freedom. For what is at stake in the confrontation with death is not whether anything survives — for that much is demonstrably clear — but whether what survives can remain itself, retain its sovereignty, and author its own destiny, rather than being processed by an alien order.

In the opening movement, I staged a confrontation between two of the most formidable figures of contemporary survival research: Jeffrey Mishlove and Stephen Braude. Mishlove marshals the full panoply of empirical evidence — NDEs, reincarnation cases, mediumship, xenoglossy, instrumental Transcommunication — into a defense of monistic idealism. Braude, with analytic rigor, insists that survival is epistemically possible but never compulsory, pointing to the omnivorous elasticity of "super-Psi" as an alternative.

Between these poles — dissolution into cosmic mentation and an unfalsifiable Psi omniscience — I drew a third path: Jamesian pluralism. This pluralism affirms a cosmos of contending minds, a battlefield of wills at every scale, where genuine novelty can emerge, where individuality is preserved, and where freedom is real. This was the metaphysical ground cleared for all that would follow.

From that ground, I turned to the empirical field where the boundaries of personhood are most radically tested: the evidence for reincarnation and possession. Stevenson's forensic documentation of children's past-life memories, complete with birthmarks and behavioral continuities, demands that something more than imagination or fraud is at work. Wambach's hypnotic regressions extend the case to statistical scale. Yet cases of abrupt personality replacement — Sumitra/Shiva, Veena/Ramoo — press the issue beyond reincarnation into possession.

Braude's analogies to dissociation and mediumship suggest that these categories are not mutually exclusive. Rather, we inhabit a spectrum where identities can overlay, merge, bifurcate, and cohabit. The Jamison twins hint that even one soul may be instantiated in two bodies at once, just as multiple personalities may inhabit a single body. Here the self is revealed not as an indivisible atom but as a composite pattern, capable of ingress and egress across thresholds of embodiment. The ontology of personhood is porous and pluralistic.

If the first two chapters dismantled the false alternatives of materialist annihilation and monistic absorption, the third tore away the consoling veils of religious eschatology. The near-death tunnel, the light, the panoramic life review — these are not sacraments of grace but technologies of control. Monroe's testimony of the loosh farm, Atwater's unexpurgated taxonomy of NDEs, and the dramaturgical masquerades of the abduction canon converge upon a single conclusion: the afterlife, as ordinarily encountered, is a psychotronic bureaucracy.

The archons wear masks — angels, elders, greys — but their function is the same: to extract, recycle, and return us. Heaven and hell are two wings of the same prison. The Moon itself appears as a spectral turbine, lensing and harvesting soul-energy for a wider economy. Liberation begins not in going into the Light but in refusing it, in anamnesis rather than lethe, in revolt rather than submission. The Promethean path is disclosure — aletheia as remembrance — that reclaims the soul from inventory status and prepares it for insurgent navigation.

To make sense of this theater, I advanced a radical yet inevitable thesis: the soul is an informational architecture, a persisting configuration of executable code within a quantum computational cosmos. Building upon Shannon, Landauer, Wheeler, and Vopson, I argued that information is physical, that it carries mass, and that physics itself reveals its underlying logic as code.

This ontology reframes every survival phenomenon: reincarnation is reinstallation, possession is an overlay, bilocation is concurrent instancing, and xenoglossy is the activation of dormant subroutines. Even the Mandela Effect discloses itself as a version-control artifact, a rollback or branch merge in the simulation. Prophecy becomes intelligible as interaction with the forecast engine of the system. The Akashic Record is a literal data library, not mystical metaphor. In this framework, Atlantis appears less a myth than a record of informational catastrophe: the mass of human data production tipping geophysical balance.

What emerges is a Promethean imperative: if the soul is software, then the task is not merely to endure, but instead to seize authorship — to learn to fork, merge, and port ourselves into futures of our own design.

Against this backdrop, I passed the inherited eschatologies of Greece, Jerusalem, Mecca, India, and Tibet through the fire of empirical survival data. Wherever they remembered anamnesis, graded ascent, or participatory authorship, they aligned with the evidence. Wherever they installed courts, cages, or eternal damnation, they betrayed it.

Orphic tablets, with their commands to shun Lethe and drink Mnemosyne, preserved the essence of anamnesis. The Platonic myth of Er dramatized judgment, choice, and forgetting, but mistook the realm for bodiless Forms. Biblical resurrectional eschatology foresaw continuity, yet devolved into juridical theater. The Gnostics alone grasped the prison-like function of the cosmos, though they lacked the technics for insurgency. Islam codified the most rigid closure: sealed barzakh, courtroom cosmos, eternal hell — untenable in light of the porous, iterative, and informational realities we now know.

Hinduism, in its modern synthesis, flirted with simulation metaphors but clung to dualism. Buddhism, by contrast, with its *anatta* and *bardos*, came closest to a process ontology: a pattern-based continuum of informational re-instantiation. Read psychotronically, the Tibetan *Book of the Dead* becomes a manual of programmable *bardos*, and its peaceful and wrathful deities are dramaturgical masks to be recognized and dissolved.

The verdict is clear: religions are not merely false or true. They are hybrid. Where they align with Promethean anamnesis, they preserve fragments of truth. Where they serve archontic order, they become masks of control.

The culmination of *Thanosis* is not metaphysical speculation, but tactical preparation. Survival without sovereignty is livestock survival. To endure as an agent beyond death requires training, discipline, and *techne*.

The sixth and final chapter demonstrates that the passage through death is not a mystery to be venerated nor an inevitability to be endured, but a process to be mastered. By weaving together Monroe's field-tested psychotronic drills, Gallimore's neurophenomenological cartography of the World Space, Gurdjieff's lunar cosmology, the symbolic consoles disclosed by Hieronymus, and Raikov's directed reincarnation, it establishes that the afterlife is not an amorphous hereafter, but a structured machinery designed for harvest, sedation, and recycling. The difference between being processed as fodder and persisting as an agent lies in discipline: the training to stabilize vibratory carriers, to vectorize affect, to deploy idents and rotes, to read and seize symbolic machines, and to install identities with lucidity rather than submit to imposed templates. Death is revealed as the ultimate switch in a manifold of possible worlds, a forced displacement that either consigns us to domestication or opens onto sovereign navigation. The conclusion of this work is that thanotic mastery is not only possible but imperative: to confront the machinery of death with Promethean craft, to refuse the harvest, and to transform the *bardo* from prison into passage.

At the heart of my Philosophy of the Future lies the recognition that Being itself is spectral. To say that Being is spectral is to deny the ultimacy of every binary that has organized metaphysical thought since the Greeks: life versus death, spirit versus matter, truth versus illusion, natural versus artificial. The afterlife is not an "otherworld" opposed to this one, but a dimension of the spectrum of existence that interpenetrates the visible world at every point. What parapsychology has shown, through rigorously controlled studies of telepathy, precognition, and mediumship, is that the psyche is not localized in the brain but is distributed across the informational field of the cosmos itself.

Survival of consciousness after bodily death is not a miraculous exception to nature; it is an ontological disclosure of the spectral essence of nature. If psyche persists beyond the organism, then life and death are revealed to be phases of a continuum. The human being is not an encapsulated subject trapped in a decaying body but a spectral node in an informational cosmos — one that can reconfigure, reincarnate, or persist in other dimensions of experience. Recognition of this truth would constitute the most radical ontological revolution in history, one that makes Copernicus and Darwin appear as mere preludes.

The epistemological significance of psychical research lies not merely in the addition of a new set of anomalies to be explained within a revised scientific framework, but in the revelation that all frameworks are spectral projections. Thomas Kuhn was correct to see that scientific paradigms are politically and socially conditioned, but he still imagined that we remain confined to one paradigm at a time. The real import of parapsychology is that it reveals the constructedness of every paradigm, and thus opens the possibility of a *post-paradigmatic science*, a science that consciously plays with multiple frameworks simultaneously.

Psychotronics is the decisive example here. The Soviet attempt to develop psychic capacities as operational technologies shows us that extrasensory perception and psychokinesis are not "miracles" but techniques — *technai* in the Greek sense — that can be cultivated, systematized, and engineered. To see this is to recognize that science is not a mirror of nature but a mode of *mekhane*, of cunningly enframing reality so as to render it manipulable. Epistemology, when confronted with the evidence of survival and Psychotronics, must accept that knowledge is never about an "objective reality" behind appearances, but always about the construction of worlds of experience that are pragmatically useful.

The most destabilizing consequence of the Spectral Revolution is political. All forms of authority since the dawn of civilization have relied on death as the ultimate limit, the final horizon around which power is organized. Religion legitimates power by promising salvation or damnation after death. The State mobilizes men to kill and die in war by making death the price of loyalty. Even secular ideologies depend on the finitude of human life to justify sacrifice for the collective. But if consciousness persists after bodily death — and if Psychotronics furnishes us with the means to explore, communicate, and perhaps even organize beyond the veil — then death ceases to be the foundation of political order. The afterlife becomes a contested domain of power. Imagine what it would mean for intelligence agencies to develop reliable means of communication with the dead, or for dissidents to continue their resistance from the other side. The nation-state system would not survive the discovery that sovereignty extends beyond the grave. Politics would be spectralized: a struggle between the living and the dead, the incarnate and the discarnate, over the very definition of humanity's future.

This is why entrenched powers resist Parapsychology with such vehemence. The Spectral Revolution would demand a restructuring of society more radical than any political revolution in history. It would not simply replace one regime with another but overthrow the metaphysical monopoly of death itself.

To call Psychotronics a "technology of the soul" is not metaphorical but literal. If technology is understood in its primordial Greek sense of *techne* and *mekhane*, then the cultivation of telepathic, precognitive, and psychokinetic abilities is as technological as metallurgy or electronics. Indeed, it is more fundamental since it reveals the spectral essence of all technology as projection and enframing.

The Soviet Union's investment in Psychotronics was not an eccentric diversion; rather, it was an anticipation of the next phase of technoscience. While Western parapsychologists were marginalized and mocked, the Soviets sought to weaponize the spectral. They understood that psychic phenomena, if real, would revolutionize warfare, intelligence, and governance. But the real stakes are even higher: Psychotronics is the key to evolving human consciousness itself, regaining at a higher level the intuitive capacities that atrophied with the rise of technical reason.

The Spectral Revolution is thus not only an epistemological and political upheaval — it is also a technological one. It demands that we develop Psychotronics not as curiosities or weapons, but as Promethean tools to consciously guide our evolution. If we fail to do so, others will — and they will use them to enslave us, reducing human beings to mere standing-reserve in a spectral Matrix.

At the deepest level, the Spectral Revolution is an eschatological event. To validate the afterlife scientifically is to end the reign of death. Not that death will cease as a biological process, but it will no longer be experienced as the ultimate horizon of existence. The terror of death has been the foundation of religion, morality, and politics for millennia. Its collapse would mean the collapse of every order founded on it. But the end of death is also the beginning of true freedom. If consciousness persists, then each of us is already spectral, already more than mortal. To know this is to stand within history as

Prometheus, unbound at last, bearing fire from beyond the grave. The afterlife is not a static heaven or hell, but a frontier of exploration, an open horizon of becoming. Psychotronics is the vessel with which we can navigate that frontier, the craft that allows us to cross the threshold and return with knowledge.

The significance of the afterlife for the Spectral Revolution, then, is nothing less than the disclosure of humanity's superhuman destiny. To recognize that psyche persists beyond the body is to realize that evolution does not end with death, that our becoming is not bounded by biology but continues into spectral dimensions. This recognition is the very essence of the Philosophy of the Future: a philosophy that dares to affirm the spectral as the matrix of our freedom, and to wield Psychotronics as the craft by which we transfigure ourselves into architects of a world where life and death, matter and spirit, technology and magic, are revealed as moments of a single spectral continuum.

BIBLIOGRAPHY

Atwater, P.M.H. *Beyond the Light: The Mysteries and Revelations of Near-Death Experiences*. New York: Avon Books, 1995.

Beloff, J.S. "Psi Phenomena: Causal Versus Acausal Interpretation." *Journal of the Society for Psychical Research* 49 (1977): 573–582.

Bostrom, Nick. "Are You Living in a Computer Simulation?" *Philosophical Quarterly* 53, no. 211 (2003): 243–255.

Braude, Stephen E. *ESP and Psychokinesis: A Philosophical Examination*. Philadelphia: Temple University Press, 1979.

———. *First Person Plural: Multiple Personality and the Philosophy of Mind*. Revised ed. Lanham, MD: Rowman & Littlefield, 1995.

———. *Immortal Remains: The Evidence for Life After Death*. Lanham, MD: Rowman & Littlefield, 2003.

Britannica Editors. "Mandela Effect." *Encyclopaedia Britannica*. Accessed 2025. https://www.britannica.com/science/Mandela-effect.

Cranston, Sylvia, and Carey Williams Head. *Reincarnation in World Thought*. New York: Philosophical Library, 1967.

Evans-Wentz, W.Y., ed. *The Tibetan Book of the Dead (Bardo Thödol)*. 1927. Reprint, Oxford: Oxford University Press, 2000.

Fowler, Raymond E. *The Andreasson Affair: The True Story of a Close Encounter of the Fourth Kind*. Pompton Plains, NJ: New Page Books, 2015.

Gallimore, Andrew. *Reality Switch Technologies: Psychedelics as Tools for the Discovery and Exploration of New Worlds* (Strange Worlds Press, 2022).

Gauquelin, Michel. *Cosmic Influences on Human Behavior: The Planetary Factors in Personality*. Sedona, AZ: Aurora Press, 1985.

Gleick, James. *Chaos: Making a New Science*. New York: Penguin, 2008.

Goldberg, Bruce. *Past Lives, Future Lives Revealed*. Pompton Plains, NJ: New Page Books, 2004.

Gurdjieff, G.I. *Beelzebub's Tales*. Reprint of 1950 text. London: Penguin Arkana, 1999.

Haraldsson, Erlendur. "Children Claiming Past-Life Memories: Four Cases in Sri Lanka." *Journal of the Society for Psychical Research* 53, no. 803 (1986): 339–355.

James, William. *A Pluralistic Universe*. New York: Longmans, Green and Co., 1958.

———. *Pragmatism and the Meaning of Truth*. Cambridge, MA: Harvard University Press, 1978.

Jamison, Terry, and Linda Jamison. *Separated at Earth*. Bangor, ME: Booklocker, 2007.

Jorjani, Jason Reza. "Free Will vs. Logical Determinism." In *Lovers of Sophia*, 201–218. London: Arktos, 2019.

———. "A Critique of Shi'ite Esotericism." In *Lovers of Sophia*, 89–112. London: Arktos, 2019.

———. *Prometheism*. London: Arktos, 2020.

———. *Philosophy of the Future*. London: Arktos, 2024.

———. *Metapolemos*. London: Arktos, 2025.

Jung, C.G. *Synchronicity: An Acausal Connecting Principle*. Princeton: Princeton University Press, 2010.

Kastrup, Bernardo. *The Idea of the World: A Multi-disciplinary Argument for the Mental Nature of Reality*. Winchester, UK: Iff Books, 2019.

Keil, Jürgen, and Ian Stevenson. "Do Cases of the Reincarnation Type Show Similar Features Over Many Years? A Study of Turkish Cases a Generation Apart." *Journal of Scientific Exploration* 14, no. 2 (2000): 189–202.

Landauer, Rolf. "Irreversibility and Heat Generation in the Computing Process." *IBM Journal of Research and Development* 5, no. 3 (1961): 183–191.

McMoneagle, Joseph. *The Ultimate Time Machine*. Rocky Mount, NC: Crossroad Press, 2012.

Mishlove, Jeffrey. *Beyond the Brain: The Survival of Human Consciousness After Permanent Bodily Death*. London: BICS, 2022.

Mishlove, Jeffrey, and Brendan Engen. "Archetypal Synchronistic Resonance: A New Theory of Paranormal Experience." *Journal of Humanistic Psychology* 47, no. 2 (2007): 223–242.

Monroe, Robert A. *Journeys Out of the Body*. Garden City, NY: Doubleday, 1971. Reprint, New York: Broadway Books, 2001.

———. *Far Journeys*. Garden City, NY: Doubleday, 1985.

Ostrander, Sheila, and Lynn Schroeder. *Psychic Discoveries*. New York: Marlowe & Company, 1997.

Ouspensky, P.D. *In Search of the Miraculous: Fragments of an Unknown Teaching*. New York: Harcourt/Harvest, 2001.

Playfair, Guy Lyon. *Twin Telepathy: The Psychic Connection*. Stroud, UK: The History Press, 2008.

Redfern, Nick. *Final Events and the Secret Government Group on Demonic UFOs and the Afterlife*. San Antonio, TX: Anomalist Books, 2010.

Ring, Kenneth. "Precognitive and Prophetic Visions in Near-Death Experiences." *Anabiosis: The Journal of Near-Death Studies* 3, no. 2 (1983): 47–74.

———. "Prophetic Visions in 1988: A Critical Reappraisal." *Journal of Near-Death Studies* 9, no. 1 (1990): 1–17.

Shannon, Claude E., and Warren Weaver. *The Mathematical Theory of Communication*. Urbana: University of Illinois Press, 1971.

Sheldrake, Rupert. *Morphic Resonance: The Nature of Formative Causation*. Rochester, VT: Park Street Press, 2009.

Skeptical Inquirer Editors. "The Mandela Effect and the Science of False Memories." *Skeptical Inquirer* 45, no. 3 (2021): 36–42.

Stevenson, Ian. *Twenty Cases Suggestive of Reincarnation*. 2nd ed. Charlottesville: University of Virginia Press, 1974.

———. *Xenoglossy: A Review and Report of a Case*. Charlottesville: University Press of Virginia, 1974.

———. *Where Reincarnation and Biology Intersect*. Westport, CT: Praeger, 1997.

———. *European Cases of the Reincarnation Type*. Jefferson, NC: McFarland, 2008.

Stevenson, Ian, and Antonia Mills, eds. *Biographical Accounts of Reincarnation Cases*. Jefferson, NC: McFarland, 1994.

Stine, Harry. *Amazing and Wonderful Mind Machines You Can Build*. Prescott, AZ: Top of the Mountain Publishing, 1997.

Strieber, Anne, and Whitley Strieber. *The Communion Letters*. New York: Walker and Collier, 2003.

Strieber, Whitley. *Solving the Communion Enigma: What Is To Come*. New York: Tarcher Penguin, 2012.

Tarnas, Richard. *Prometheus the Awakener*. Putnam, CT: Spring Publications, 2018.

Thompson, Richard L. *Alien Identities: Ancient Insights into Modern UFO Phenomena*. Badger, WV: Govardhan Hill Publishing, 1995.

———. *MAYA: The World as Virtual Reality*. Badger, WV: Govardhan Hill Publishing, n.d.

Tucker, Jim B. *Life Before Life: A Scientific Investigation of Children's Memories of Previous Lives*. New York: St. Martin's Press, 2005.

Turner, Karla. *Into the Fringe*. Amazon Kindle, 1992.

———. *Taken*. Amazon Kindle, 1994.

———. *Masquerade of Angels*. Amazon Kindle, 1994.

Virk, Rizwan. *The Simulation Hypothesis*. San Francisco: Bayview Books, 2019.

Vopson, Melvin M. *Reality Reloaded: The Scientific Case for a Simulated Universe*. IPI Publishing, 2023.

Weiss, Brian. *Same Soul, Many Bodies*. London: Piatkus, 2004.

Wheeler, John Archibald. "Information, Physics, Quantum: The Search for Links." In Wojciech H. Zurek, ed., *Complexity, Entropy, and the Physics of Information*. Santa Fe Institute Studies in the Sciences of Complexity, vol. VIII. Redwood City, CA: Addison-Wesley, 1990, 3–28.

Wambach, Helen. *Reliving Past Lives: The Evidence Under Hypnosis*. London: White Crow Books, 2021.

OTHER BOOKS PUBLISHED BY ARKTOS

OTHER BOOKS PUBLISHED BY ARKTOS

OTHER BOOKS PUBLISHED BY ARKTOS

LUDWIG KLAGES	*The Biocentric Worldview*
	Cosmogonic Reflections
	The Science of Character
ANDREW KORYBKO	*Hybrid Wars*
PIERRE KREBS	*Guillaume Faye: Truths & Tributes*
	Fighting for the Essence
JULIEN LANGELLA	*Catholic and Identitarian*
HENRI LEVAVASSEUR	*Identity: The Foundation of the City*
JOHN BRUCE LEONARD	*The New Prometheans*
DIANA PANCHENKO	*The Inevitable*
JEAN-YVES LE GALLOU	*The Propaganda Society*
STEPHEN PAX LEONARD	*The Ideology of Failure*
	Travels in Cultural Nihilism
WILLIAM S. LIND	*Reforging Excalibur*
	Retroculture
PENTTI LINKOLA	*Can Life Prevail?*
GIORGIO LOCCHI	*Definitions*
H. P. LOVECRAFT	*The Conservative*
NORMAN LOWELL	*Imperium Europa*
RICHARD LYNN	*Sex Differences in Intelligence*
	A Tribute to Helmut Nyborg (ed.)
JOHN MACLUGASH	*The Return of the Solar King*
CHARLES MAURRAS	*The Future of the Intelligentsia &*
	For a French Awakening
GRAEME MAXTON	*The Follies of the Western Mind*
JOHN HARMON MCELROY	*Agitprop in America*
MICHAEL O'MEARA	*Guillaume Faye and the Battle of Europe*
	New Culture, New Right
MICHAEL MILLERMAN	*Beginning with Heidegger*
DMITRY MOISEEV	*The Philosophy of Italian Fascism*
MAURICE MURET	*The Greatness of Elites*
BRIAN ANSE PATRICK	*The NRA and the Media*
	Rise of the Anti-Media
	The Ten Commandments of Propaganda
	Zombology
TITO PERDUE	*The Bent Pyramid*
	Journey to a Location
	Lee
	Morning Crafts
	Philip
	The Sweet-Scented Manuscript
	William's House (vol. 1–4)
JOHN K. PRESS	*The True West vs the Zombie Apocalypse*
RAIDO	*A Handbook of Traditional Living* (vol. 1–2)
P R REDDALL	*Towards Awakening*
CLAIRE RAE RANDALL	*The War on Gender*
STEVEN J. ROSEN	*The Agni and the Ecstasy*
	The Jedi in the Lotus
NICHOLAS ROONEY	*Talking to the Wolf*

OTHER BOOKS PUBLISHED BY ARKTOS